Praise for Th

D1291292

"Kellan has taken the core principles of Spiritual Psychology and distilled them into a simple, practical toolset that anyone can use to transform their lives."

ORVEL RAY WILSON, CSP, best-selling author and award-winning international speaker

"To have a clear sense of the tools it takes to control your life is a wonderful thing. The ability to listen to others and see clearly where they could improve is also a good thing. However, the ability to convey to others all the tools or context needed to improve their own life, that is a magnificent gift that Kellan Fluckiger has given us in *The Book of Context*. No matter where you are in your journey, it's a must-read. Kellan is a splendid business coach, and now we know, a gifted writer."

DAVID LANCE SCHWARTZ, CEO and lead designer, DLNY

"Kellan is fearless! His ability to turn adversity into a blueprint for success is amazing. Buy this book, understand your context, and thrive!"

WINTON CHURCHILL, Founder of Barefoot Consultants

"If you want to create your best life, you will need to take fierce ownership over your will. Kellan Fluckiger's new book, *The Book of Context*, takes you through processes that help you discover a more advantageous way of living. I recommend that you get this book, follow the guidelines, and enthusiastically create your bold and courageous life now!"

KATHY MASON, best-selling author, conscious publicist and online marketing expert

"I love *The Book of* Context! As a promoter of conscious living, I understand that we are always choosing and creating our lives. *The Book of Context*, extraordinarily written and simply presented, gives eye-opening information and powerful processes, which when practiced and applied, will help the old you get out of the way, and the new you create the life you desire. Thank you, Kellan, for sharing this powerful life creation guide."

TRYNA LEE COOPER, Truly Live Consciously

"*The Book of Context* is about taking back control of your life, knowing how to exercise your true personal power, and becoming happier and more successful at anything you want to do. Don't fret about what it's titled. Just read it, embrace it, and experience all the many benefits Kellan would love for you to have."

**MORT ORMAN, M.D., best-selling author of
The 14 Day Stress Cure and stress elimination expert**

THE BOOK
OF CONTEXT

The Book of Context

Break Free from the Past – Live Powerfully in the Present –
Create an Amazing Future

Kellan Fluckiger

RED AUSSIE
— PUBLISHING —

The Book of Context
Break Free From the Past, Live Powerfully in the Present, Create
an Amazing Future

Copyright © 2018 by **Kellan Fluckiger**

Published in Phoenix, Arizona, by Red Aussie Publishing
22424 S Ellsworth Loop Rd
Unit 898
Queen Creek, AZ 85142

Contact the Publisher: RedAussiePublishing@gmail.com
www.RedAussiePublishing.com

Contact the author:
www.KellanFluckiger.com

ISBN: 978-1-7328588-0-0

Cover Design and Interior Design by Joy Fluckiger

Table of Contents

FOREWORD

My name is Dr. Mort Orman. I am an Internal Medicine physician, a wellness consultant, and a stress elimination expert.

I am truly honored to write this foreword for Kellan Fluckiger's new book, *The Book of Context*.

I've come to know Kellan very well over the past few years. I've attended some of the talks and workshops he's conducted. I've hired him to coach me on some personal and business issues, like improving my online presence and constructing a TEDx talk on stress relief for high school students.

I've also read other books he has written, all of which are excellent.

Three things impress me about Kellan: his heart, his commitment to others, and his honesty. He is a sage man and an excellent mentor.

I've been fortunate to have many wonderful mentors in my life. They included my favorite childhood uncle who became a world-renowned cardiologist, several key physicians who helped me during my medical training to become a good and successful doctor, and a very skilled psychotherapist who helped me learn about myself and my unconscious mind, to still another skilled psychiatrist who first introduced me to the power of "context."

This psychiatrist Robert Shaw, M.D., created a school for practicing psychotherapists called the Contextual Therapy Institute.

He and his wife also co-founded and co-ran a treatment center in Berkeley, California called the Contextual Therapy Center.

I know a good mentor when I see one, and Kellan is one of the best.

He's one of those rare individuals who listens so well, understands human beings so deeply, and observes our speaking, labeling, and self-limiting behaviors so observantly, that whenever he points out something that I may be doing (unknowingly), I immediately assume he's probably right.

So why did he feel compelled to write this book about context, why did he call it The Book of Context even though most people won't know what that means, and why do I think you should both read it and heed it?

Quite frankly, I didn't know much about what the term "context" meant when I first heard it years ago, especially when it was used to explain both normal and abnormal human functioning as well as human growth and development.

It had to be explained to me, and the full meaning didn't sink in immediately. Over the years, I've become more and more comfortable with the term and have found it to have tremendous implications, for me both personally and professionally.

In this book, Kellan is mainly focusing on our many and diverse self-limiting beliefs. If there is a book that can help you master this incredibly challenging aspect of our lives, this is it.

Kellan is a master truth-teller, so there is an enormous amount of truth and wisdom throughout this book. You will not only learn why you have self-limiting beliefs but how to both identify them and then break free of them.

More importantly, you will learn that you actually *can* do this. It takes work and effort, which Kellan guides you through, but it is totally within your power. Only you—and your self-limiting beliefs—can stop you!

I told Kellan initially that I didn't like the title he chose for this book. I was pretty sure most people wouldn't understand what he meant by "context" and therefore wouldn't feel compelled to pick it up, much less read it.

I recently read *The Book Of Joy*, by the Dalai Lama and Desmond Tutu. Now there's a title most people can instantly understand. However, *The Book Of Context*? Not a winner. Kellan was determined to stick with this title. In a way, it is perfect.

You see, words and titles don't have meanings by themselves. Somebody always must supply you with the intended background context. With some words like "joy," we all pretty much understand the context behind the word.

But not always. For example, Kellan's wife—who is also a wonderful and deeply caring person—happens to be named Joy. Unless I give you this context, you would have no way of knowing that's who I meant when I used the very same word.

However, a word like "context" can mean a great many things. As the author, Kellan is free to create any meaning he wants, as long as he informs you, the reader, as you go along.

Kellan and I have a slightly different understanding of what the term "context" means for human development and mastering our innate personal powers. But that's OK, because that's how words work, and that's how human beings communicate and share ideas.

So just as both Kellan and I have the natural human capacity to choose our preferred meanings for any specific term we use, you too have this same natural ability. We all can choose and reshape the contexts of our lives.

We can update and improve contexts that expand our health and well-being. We can update the contexts we choose for our relationships, our happiness, and even our ultimate contentment.

We can create contexts that can help us eliminate most of our stress. The point is, we don't have as many limits as we think we do. Also, most of the limits we think we have are not real.

The Book of Context is about taking back control of your life, knowing how to exercise your true personal power, and becoming happier and more successful at anything you want to do.

Don't fret about the title. Just read it, embrace it, and experience all the many benefits Kellan would love for you to have.

I applaud you Kellan for having the courage and commitment to writing this book, and to "telling it like it is." You have once again brought something new, wonderful, powerful, and helpful to the world. Just as you always do.

INTRODUCTION

It's not often you receive an entire book, complete with content and instructions for use all at once. At least it doesn't happen that way to me.

However, it happened that way with this book. In my near-death experience in June 2018, at the University of Alberta Hospital, I had three conversations with God at the doorway between life and eternity.

In the second of these conversations, this entire concept and framework were given to me so thoroughly and powerfully that twelve days later when I was brought out of sedation, and back to consciousness, I could remember it precisely.

Interestingly enough, I have two completely different feelings as I write this book. First, I'm excited because I know of its power and that it will be useful to those who apply it.

Second, like any creative bringing forth a work of art, I sit with a nervous pit in my stomach wondering if it will be understood, accepted, and used, or misunderstood, rejected and ridiculed.

I decided to go ahead and write the book because these truths have been and remain a dominant force for change in my life. They have also helped many clients understand how to get unstuck from stories that come from the past.

Furthermore, this book will bring great clarity and understanding of what limits our thinking and actions, and why we insist that we can or cannot do certain things.

Also, this book will give you a key to create a future that is exactly what you want. Let me be clear on this point. YOU have the power in your hands to create a future that is precisely what you want to have.

The principal reason we don't create that future we imagine is quite simply because we do not believe we can. We stay stuck in stories of weakness and inability instead of breaking through to the truth.

I hope that with this book in hand, you start changing that today.

PROLOGUE
OUTER SPACE

When I was a kid, we talked about "outer space" in the most reverent tones. It was that place where anything was possible, where monsters dwelt, and magical things happened. Aliens with superpowers were everywhere, and they were always more powerful and developed than we were.

We had endless fantasies about this mystical realm as we devoured science-fiction books and eagerly watched movies and television shows all based on the fertile imaginations of those who shared our unusual perceptions of the unknown.

The woman was hunched over the stove, preparing dinner. Judging by the manner of dress and the decor of the house, or at least the kitchen where she worked, it must've been the late 1800s or early 1900s.

Her husband came in from outside, dressed in overalls and a crude hat. He had been working on the farm with the animals that sustained their existence.

They greeted each other, and he sat down at the table, waiting for his dinner. They exchanged some small talk about how the day had gone and a problem with one of the animals.

They were speaking English, so it appeared that the setting was rural America, most likely in the timeframe I mentioned earlier.

Suddenly, they both grew quiet and stared at each other. There was some scratching in the attic that concerned them. Nothing in the attic should be making a noise like that.

Perhaps a big rat was up there scrabbling for food. Maybe a bird had come in through the gable window that stood open in the night sky.

However, the sound was too loud and out of place. They both got worried and a bit scared. They had no idea what they should do next.

The scene cut to the inside of a very modern spaceship. The captain of the spacecraft was radioing a distress call back to their home base. Passing through a cosmic storm, they had become lost.

After the storm passed, they found themselves within the visual range of a planet. Knowing that damage must be repaired and seeking a place to do it, they had gone ahead and moved into orbit around that planet.

The three-person crew piloted the vessel into a gigantic alien structure that seemed abandoned. After assessing the suitability of the atmosphere, the team realized it was breathable. One of the three went outside to assess the damage to the spacecraft.

The man outside was having trouble grasping the enormous scale of the structure and was having a struggle describing it to his two shipmates on the inside.

They decided that things were safe enough, and with extreme caution and the appearance that everything was long abandoned, they agreed they should stay to make repairs.

Cutting back to the kitchen scene, the farmer told his wife he would get a shotgun and go up and see what the noise in the attic could be.

After the farmer left the room, the noise intensified, and the woman became impatient. Deciding that her husband was taking too long to get the gun, she picked up a rolling pin and decided to take matters into her own hands.

After all, she reasoned whatever was in the attic couldn't be that big of a deal. She walked across the room, pulled down the stairway that led upwards and began to ascend the stairs.

The scene cut back to the spaceship. The outer door of the spacecraft was opened again, and the two remaining crew members were carefully descending to the surface of the gigantic alien structure.

The woman finished climbing the stairs and began to move across the room to where she believed she heard the noise.

Across the room, she saw a tiny object on the floor that was no more than an inch or two tall. Taking courage from its small size, she moved toward it. Clearly, she could not understand how such a tiny object made any noise at all, let alone enough to cause concern.

The camera zoomed in on the tiny object. As the shot got very tight, it was clear that the small object was a spacecraft. Emblazoned on the side was a familiar sight.

The emblem was instantly recognizable. It was the Stars & Stripes accompanied by the familiar name "United States of America."

The sudden revelation shocked me and completely changed everything that I had been thinking and believing as I watched the television show.

Those who remember this series will not be surprised. Such suspense and unexpected shocks were a regular feature on "The Twilight Zone."

"If you want to make a Difference...

start from a place of Truth

Live from a place of Truth

Truth carries its own Power."

Kellan Fluckiger

WE ARE WHAT WE BELIEVE - WE GET WHAT WE EXPECT

We have all had the experience of having a surprising revelation in real life that completely shifts our perception and understanding of a given situation.

In the prologue story, I believed I was on earth in rural America on some remote farm. I believed that the visitors are aliens and were about to wreak some havoc on the poor unsuspecting farmers.

Everything in the set up was designed to make my thinking go in that direction. I was worried about the farmers, thinking that the aliens would have some death ray and be scheming to take over the world, starting right then and there.

Imagine my shock and surprise to realize that the visitors were space travelers from America who had somehow landed on a planet with people a thousand times bigger than they were.

This is a simple example from a suspense-filled story carefully crafted to provide suspense and shock. Also, it was intentionally structured to make us think and realize that what we believe to be true is rarely accurate.

In a more personal and practical example, I experienced a profound change in my most important personal relationship by asking one simple question. A bit of background will help you understand.

I grew up with physical and emotional abuse that left me with an intense belief that I was inadequate. Somehow, I was broken, and everything I did was usually wrong. This assumption colored everything about my relationship with people and life.

I also experienced depression off-and-on for over four decades. It was undiagnosed and untreated and consequently, all the more devastating.

Part of the abusive upbringing was isolation, including never discussing personal problems. This was the reason that my condition went all those decades without diagnosis or treatment. I mistakenly believed that my brokenness was all *my* fault and mine alone to suffer.

This led me on a tortured path of broken relationships, addictions, and similar problems typical of this situation.

Eventually, God sent me an angel. I was fortunate enough to find my wife, Joy. Amazingly, in another stroke of divine intervention, she agreed to marry me. She is fantastic, and I was determined to create a great relationship.

Joy is a direct woman, who says what she thinks, without unkindness, but also without excess fluff. For me, a person with terrible self-esteem at the beginning of our relationship, this always felt dangerous.

Because I always assumed everything was my fault, and all mistakes and misunderstandings originated with me, she would often say something that would emotionally trigger me, and I would have an outsized defensive emotional reaction.

Not understanding my emotion, she asked me why I had such strong negative reactions. I felt like she was passive-aggressive. My immediate and sometimes sarcastic answer was, "What else could you possibly mean by those words. I mean, anyone in their right mind who heard those words would understand that they are an attack on me?"

Her explanation that she meant no attack, and her statement was a simple question, had no effect on my feelings or on the subsequent conversation, which was generally never very productive.

One day, after years of this kind of dialogue, and much personal work, a realization came over me after precisely such a trigger. A voice in my mind said, "What if the words mean only what the words say?"

Before responding, I repeated her statement and paid attention to *only* the words. I subtracted or ignored everything else that I had created as the emotional meaning of the words.

I asked myself the magic question: "What else could this mean (besides the obvious?)"

I say, "the obvious," because with my beliefs or "context," there was only one possible meaning: the attack I had perceived.

When I dropped my assumptions and asked the question in pure curiosity, everything changed.

From that moment on, I learned to take statements and questions at face value without assigning any emotional baggage or intent.

A whole new world opened up to me. From that time on, the nature of the relationship improved dramatically.

Imagine a simple question, and a single shift in context, on my part alone, changed the game.

I began to wonder where else such a powerful and profound effect could be realized.

Chapter 1
WHAT IS A "CONTEXT?"

Context is the assigned meaning you create in any situation. It may come from many places:

- The definition and power that we attribute to the words.
- The accompanying body language and subtle facial expressions.
- The way we interpret the actions of others.
- The attitudes we interpret from those around us.
- The historical meaning of some things.
- The meaning we assign to random incidents (right place, right time.)
- The meaning we attach to the effects and outcomes caused by forces of nature, accidents, and other unexpected things.
- The current versions of the "rules and laws of science." (Remember, we used to believe the world was flat, that letting blood cured disease and that earth, air, fire, and water were the only elements. The so-called laws of science change all the time, especially when a new explanation better suited the facts.)
- Many, many other factors.

Context is the learned and assumed meaning of any given situation.

It is powerful and essential. How often have we heard that the meaning of something is changed completely when it is taken "out of context."

Another peculiar element of context is that it is always 100% based on the past. What has happened to us or others defines what everything means. It also determines what we believe will likely happen now and in the future.

For example, if we get into an accident, we assume bad luck – wrong place, wrong time.

The first piece of context is "I had bad luck." Often it'll change to "I always seem to have bad luck." Or, worse, "I must be doing something wrong because I always have bad luck."

Beyond the actual consequences of this event, we can take it even further and blame ourselves or some behavior or attitude in our past for being the magnet and source of bad luck.

Walking down the street in San Francisco after an interview where I didn't get the job I wanted, I screamed at the sky, "I never get the gig." My context was a belief that because of some failing in me, I was the person who always got the raw deal.

Someone else was always the lucky one.

Maybe someone you know wins a few million dollars in the lottery. You chafe in envy and perhaps anger, being completely aware of their failings and shortcomings as a person.

"They are such jerks, why did they get good luck and I got nothing?"

If you stop and think about it, there are thousands of examples that happen in a week, perhaps hundreds in a day where the lenses we wear about a situation, a person or life in general completely colors what we think and feel about events and the people involved.

Emotions rush through our body and cause tension, an upset stomach, and a host of other things that are the consequence of the thinking that we have. It all starts with a thought and belief.

The examples so far have been of adverse reactions to events and circumstances. Negative events seem to carry the most power because of the survival instinct in the limbic brain, and because the context of modern society is danger and negativity.

The positive assumptions and reactions are similar and come from exactly the same source and in the same way.

For example, a person gets severely ill and then has an astounding recovery.

We know their good qualities and remember the benefits that have come to us as a result of our relationship. Our reaction is that such a recovery was just and deserved, and we feel a sense of justice and happiness.

Without taking the time to give a hundred examples, context is the set of beliefs that we carry, from all sources, about the meaning of everything around us.

Often, we write these into the very fabric of our heart and soul, and without any conscious thought, they define the meaning of situations and circumstances as they occur.

Without these beliefs, events would take place all around us without any reaction or emotion on our part whatsoever.

This points to the obvious conclusion that if we wore different lenses, the same events that bring an adverse reaction with one context, could quickly generate a positive response and set of feelings in another circumstance.

This means that every experience we have is created based on the context we accept as being true. This context is woven from the beliefs we have accepted about everything that happens.

Change your beliefs, re-do your context, change your life.

Chapter 2
BELIEFS - WHAT ARE THEY?

Beliefs are those things you "know," (or think you know) about what words mean, how the world operates, and your place in that world.

We used to believe the earth was flat. The consequence of that belief was that we didn't undertake certain activities because we were confident that we would fall off the edge and into the unknown.

Another belief was that a man couldn't run a mile in less than four minutes. The human body cannot stand the stress of accomplishing this feat.

Not so long ago, learned scientists declared that there was no such thing as molecules and atoms. It was a fanciful explanation with no basis. This mistaken notion was commonly held up as truth as recently as the time of the early years of Albert Einstein.

We smile at such beliefs now and understand how they came about. At the same time, we know how misplaced they were. It's interesting to contemplate the delays in research and achievement caused by tenaciously clinging to error.

Today, we operate with a similar pile of assumptions or beliefs that do not comport with how things work. As obvious as that conclusion is, we believe that NOW we KNOW how things work, and therefore we are correct *this* time.

Pure reflection teaches us that just as we obliterated these old beliefs and replaced them with new knowledge, our current views are subject to revision and even stark adjustment as we make new discoveries.

It's easy to talk like this about scientific knowledge and things that are demonstrable in a laboratory or other visible forum.

It's much more difficult, but no less valid, that beliefs about less tangible and less visible things are also held just as tightly and at the same time are just as limiting.

Beliefs act as limitations. We try or do not try specific activities in our lives because we believe that we already know the outcomes and consequences of the effort.

We don't talk to someone because we know the conversation will be futile. We don't try something because we failed before, or someone we know says it's pointless.

An often-used theme in books and movies is that the boy never asks the girl out on a date because he believes there's no way she would accept.

The story gets interesting when a friend intervenes to help the boy see that he's wrong. There are entire movies about the pranks and lengths to which the friends go to get the date set up.

Similarly, the context you accept as truth, built from the beliefs you hold, firmly limit what you will try and define what you can accomplish in your life.

It's easy to think of endless examples that are obvious and happen every day.

It's more difficult, and undoubtedly more painful, but far more useful to examine the self-constructed "prison walls" imposed by beliefs to which we cling.

- A belief that you can't make a certain amount of money.

- A belief that you are not worthy of a particular opportunity.

- A belief that you will screw something up because you had a failure in the past.

- A belief that a certain level of success is beyond your station or more than you should be able to achieve, based on who you are and from where you came.

- A belief that you cannot learn a specific skill and that you are doomed to failure in that area.

- A belief that you are a person who is "always late."

- A belief that "that's just the way I am."

- The list is infinite.

It's comfortable to accept these beliefs because they appear woven into the very fabric of our DNA. We don't even hear ourselves say these things as we explain our situation.

However, beliefs demonstrate their power and validity over-and-over again in everyday aspects of our lives.

When we validate them with our speech and habits, they become more and more "true." The truth of this belief is confirmed each time we revisit and accept it.

The real truth is that such beliefs are a self-fulfilling prophecy and have nothing at all to do with what is possible.

Often, our set of beliefs continue to be the concrete walls that limit what we achieve, what we attempt, and ultimately, what we have as "our lot in life."

Beliefs build the context and the walls. Then we merely settle in for what we believe we can have.

Chapter 3

BELIEFS - WHERE DO THEY COME FROM?

It's impossible to list all the places where we might pick up beliefs.

However, let's talk about a few prominent examples that powerfully shape us.

Our childhood. Every child is dramatically affected by the circumstance of his or her upbringing. Some of these effects are very good and serve as a great foundation and operating system for life.

For example, I was taught at a very young age to work and to take care of myself. I had chores around the house and needed to make my way.

My friends didn't have such responsibilities, and at the time, I was jealous of them and felt my parents were unfair. In retrospect, I've learned the value of hard work and have been grateful for that work ethic all my life.

Another personal example is the strict religious upbringing I had. The religion was absolute and unquestionable. The consequences of the slightest violation were violent punishment.

I was screamed at, sworn at, and beaten excessively for violating the principles of the religion which I was expected to follow without question.

Another interesting aspect of this environment was that I never learned the difference between my parents' personal preferences and the "principles of truth."

Their preferences about everything were enforced just as harshly as the principles they deemed to be so critical and sacred.

The frequency of failure and the regularity and severity of punishment taught me a critical lesson. I was fundamentally flawed, and no matter what I did, I would never be good enough.

I accepted and internalized this belief. It had weighty consequences throughout my adult life. I was 52 years old before dramatic events unfolded that changed my course for the better, just like the friends helping the boy get the date. Finally, I was able to take off the false lenses.

Beyond these personal examples, it's not difficult to see that how a person was raised as a child, in plenty or privation, with encouragement or ridicule, with excellent teachers or indifferent instructors, dramatically affects how they feel about themselves, opportunities and life in general.

Aside from how you are raised, here is a partial list of other sources:

Friends. The attitudes, opinions, and values of your friends color what you think is real and possible. These beliefs find their way deep into your heart and soul and remain there unless, or until something happens to bring them into question, and you make a conscious decision to change them.

Culture plays an enormous role in the beliefs that we have. How we speak to others, the rules of etiquette, the roles of men and women and children, and even animals in our existence.

Music and what is deemed "good and bad" in that medium.

Conversations and topics you're "allowed" to have with others.

Aspirations that are looked on with favor and those that we frown upon.

Religion or the lack of religion is a powerful influence on what you believe. This is particularly influential because many religions, if not most, address not only behavior, consequences, and outcomes in this life but also rewards and penalties in a life that comes later.

Economic status plays a substantial role in forming beliefs. Living with the repeated refrain "I can't afford that," instead of "let's make a plan," colors not only what you think you can have, but also plays a role in what you think of others who have more or less than you do.

The **books** you read.

The **television** programs and movies that you watch.

Myths, fairy tales, and comic-book heroes, all shape what we think life is and what is possible.

Successes and failures that you experience also shape your belief in what is possible and what you may or may not "deserve."

There are many other influences that subtly or overtly shape our beliefs. Those that occur early in life tend to push their way in the furthest, and we often treat these as absolute truth.

These beliefs stay with us until other events in life either gently or rudely bring us to the truth that the earth is not flat and life does not work the way we thought it did.

The critical element here is that the beliefs that you form from all these inputs are merely that: beliefs and only beliefs. They may not be true.

Chapter 4
BELIEFS - CAN THEY BE CHANGED?

In a word, YES. The process is easy to say and sometimes very hard to do.

In the case of physical demonstrations like the earth being flat, a simple test will reveal the truth. Sail around the world and come back to where you started.

Launch a vehicle into space and observe the spherical shape and beauty of the earth beneath you.

Astronomical observation proved that Earth was not the center of the universe. Galileo was imprisoned as a heretic for claiming to have learned through his telescope that the sun was the center of the solar system and not Earth – a drastic consequence for exposing a false belief.

Things subject to physical measurement such as smashing the four-minute mile or demonstrating the existence of molecules and atoms fall into the more straightforward category.

Continued experimentation with the nature of matter then revealed protons, neutrons, and electrons. Further still, quarks are now thought to be elementary particles.

In the scientific, mathematics, and physical world, it is often simple to demonstrate the truth or falsity of many beliefs.

Some beliefs are easy to change.

However, even in the scientific world, this is not always the case. For a long time after the discovery of DNA, it was thought that the gene expression contained in the DNA was the absolute ruler of the characteristics and reactions of the living organism.

Discoveries in microbiology now indicate that there is significant differentiation in how DNA expresses itself, even in cells with precisely the same DNA, when subject to different environments.

That makes microbiologists now wonder if cells have some ability to make choices, almost the equivalent of a brain!

It is far more challenging to address and change beliefs that are not subject to physical proof.

For example:

- What we believe to be true about ourselves.

- What we hold to be self-evident about others.

- What we "know" to be real about the meaning of life, God, religion, spirituality, and the origins and purposes of the universe.

All those topics are just as real as the existence of atoms and shape the nature and power of our human experience. The nature of these beliefs makes them much more difficult to identify and change.

In our recent collective past, we shared a belief that people could not change. We have memorialized such things in sayings like "a leopard cannot change its spots."

Brain research and other work have demonstrated that this is not true. We now have a new word in the vocabulary: "neuroplasticity," which is a fancy way of saying you can change the wiring in your brain.

Suddenly, the collective belief that we cannot change our personality or our fundamental behavior and habits is no longer valid.

However, it was already false before we made these discoveries. We were just unaware of that fact and didn't push the boundaries. We didn't invent this ability of the brain by discovering it. We have merely smashed the old belief.

How many other beliefs in your context can you smash?

In scientific areas, a documented discovery makes it easy to talk about the implications of such a breakthrough. When we get personal, because our internal beliefs are so hardwired to our lives, it remains difficult to accept and make the changes that this discovery show is possible.

The fundamental truth is this: you *can* change your personality, you can change your beliefs, and you can fundamentally rewire your context, or how you look at the world. Making this change will radically alter your trajectory and life experience.

Even those things deeply branded into your heart and deeply wired into your mind can be rewired, undone, healed, and reformatted to create a different life experience for you.

You have the ability, in your own hands, with the right information and the right help, to create the life you want. It starts with understanding that you have the control switch of your beliefs and context of life firmly in your control.

It is up to you to flip the switch and immediately start creating the life you want.

Chapter 5
LABELS AND LANGUAGE

Now that we "know" through scientific research what we already knew intuitively, why is changing internal beliefs harder than changing external beliefs?

Beliefs that deal with matters of the mind and heart are often more challenging to measure and demonstrate. This makes them easier to hide, hide behind, and pretend away.

We can tell ourselves that we feel better about our relationship with ourselves, with God or with someone else. We often do that to give our conscience a little pat on the head as if to say "there, there, it's getting better."

However, the very act of pretending announces negativity and skepticism. That moves us further down the road reinforcing the belief that we can't change or won't change, and so we have to do things like telling ourselves lies to get by.

Another thing that reveals beliefs in stark relief, is the language and labels that we use. For example, if we believe that the world is unfair, we look for models that reinforce that belief, and our language gives us away in an instant.

This attitude makes us critical of others, especially when they get something awesome or have success. We also speak negatively about our opportunities or accomplishments.

Even when something goes well, or we do something

praiseworthy, we find fault with it and are quick to point out how it should have been done differently, better or sooner.

We treat pessimism as a virtue and use our outlook and expectation as justification for everything wrong that happens to us, and then we complain about life in general.

Here are some telltale signs. Do you complain about the weather? Do you complain about coworkers? Do you complain about your life partner? Do you complain about working conditions or your income or your health?

Living in the constant mode of a complaint is a telltale sign that you have a low opinion of yourself. This belief reflects itself in the constant barrage of language that goes on in your mind and your mouth.

If you choose to go on a voyage of self-discovery and potential change, start by paying attention to the language you use. Each time you find yourself being critical or using negative words, make a note in your mind, and then explore how it affects your body.

If this is a habit of yours, you will be shocked at how often the negative language occurs and the corresponding set of feelings that are your usual fare.

A hallmark of such a habit is a sincere conviction that the negativity, skepticism or bitterness that you display about life's conditions, your fortune, or others' circumstances is the only real way to interpret what you see.

This demonstrates the invisible yet awesome power of the chains of belief and context.

Another powerful indicator and reinforcement of beliefs about ourselves and others are the labels we use. For example:

- "I'm always late."

- "I am bored every time "he" talks at a meeting."

- "They always turn in shoddy work and seem to get away with it."

- "I learned to stop worrying about that; it's just the way I am."

- "I'm very disorganized and can never find anything."

All these and hundreds of similar labels are subtle or overt reinforcements of beliefs that we hold about ourselves. None of them are unchangeable or inevitable fact.

They may be precisely right as a description of the behavior you have chosen in the present, but they are not true is an absolute statement of permanent truth about your life.

Sometimes we use them as excuses because we're not interested in finding out what it would take to be different, or in spending the effort that change would require.

We restate the label over and over as if frequent repetition creates truth. It does make beliefs more challenging to change, but it doesn't establish any additional truth.

Frequent repetition of our beliefs and reinforcement of labels we attach to ourselves and others adds layers of cement to our already established walls.

Accepting and even clinging to these things as part of our identity, makes it increasingly difficult to create the possible change – if we choose to go there.

"We make things too complicated. If you have a clear vision and put the work in, you get the results."

– Kellan Fluckiger

Chapter 6

STUCK-NESS

A favorite phrase in the modern lexicon of personal development is "stuck." Countless books, seminars, and Internet courses talk about the reality and the perception of being stuck in a particular spot and what to do about it.

If you've ever gotten your vehicle stuck in the mud, you know how it is to grind gears and rev the engine only to have the wheels spin uselessly with no motion taking place.

There are at least two parts to the feeling of "being stuck." First, we have habits that can keep us in the same place. The truth of this is demonstrated by the saying, "if you always do what you've always done, then you'll always get what you've always got."

Overused and funny, but fundamentally sound and valid. The habits, behaviors, and attitudes you have right now are those that led you precisely to where you are.

In other words, whether you like it or not, or whether you believe it or not, you are exactly where you want to be. To the extent you continue with the same habits, behaviors, and attitudes, you will stay in the same place.

A dominant belief that keeps us stuck is failing to acknowledge one fundamental truth. **It is our habits, behaviors, and attitudes that have brought us where we are.** We continually want to point fingers in other directions as if the circumstance or others' behavior is the cause.

Another powerful belief that keeps us stuck is the feeling *that we cannot change*. We cling to a false notion that there are fundamental things about us or our circumstances that are beyond our influence.

Our internal dialogue and external language reinforce this belief, which is another form of labeling that we talked about in the last chapter.

The reality is that *everything is subject to change*. Change is the nature of life itself. The idea that you can't change or that your circumstances can't be influenced isn't accurate.

Often this attitude about the impossibility of change is a camouflage for the fact that we won't put the required effort into the situation to create any meaningful change.

The second truth about "stuck-ness" is that *we can quickly and easily become addicted to the feeling of staying where we are*. We pretend that we're trying to make something different happen, but it's not a full-on effort.

Telltale signs of this can be:

- Procrastination.

- Failing to get the information, we need to make something happen.

- Failing to find the help required to address whatever the barriers are in your way.

- Pretending we don't have time to get it done.

- Trying halfheartedly and then defaulting quickly to our comfortable position of failure.

We become addicted to the drama and story that we "are where we are" and can't change.

We might fear change, we might be unwilling to walk into the unknown of a new future, but the truth is *never* that it can't be done.

We have even memorialized this kind of hesitation with sayings like "better the devil you know than the one you don't."

More than one person has come to me as a coach for help claiming that their goal is to make more money. In discussions about strategies and options based on their skills and desires, I hear, "I can't make too much money, or I will lose such and such benefits that I get now."

They have institutionalized stuckness and live in a world where fear of losing something they have now wholly counteracts any desire to change and negates any faith they have in a future opportunity.

They have become comfortable living in a degree of poverty. Not just poverty concerning money, but personal power and creativity. They have chosen to use their precious right of self-determination, and growth to stay where they are and then complain.

Being stuck is a story. Like all stories, you are in the middle of it, and you are where you are right now. You have the opportunity to write the future blank pages any way you want.

It is only the continued repetition and enactment of existing beliefs that keep you powerless to change and permanently stuck where you are.

The good news is that being stuck is not permanent. The moment you own your power and truly step into the opportunity to create your future, beliefs can change, and your new context can be used to mold the future you want.

Chapter 7

DANGERS OF CHANGING BELIEFS

We know what beliefs are, they are:

- The boundaries of what we think is possible.
- The ideas that we imbue with the truth.
- The boundaries we put around every situation.
- The meaning of the circumstances in the world.

We know where a belief originates. From the moment of birth until the present, our perceptions of the world around us and all the multiple inputs we receive create and shape our beliefs. The beliefs we hold form our context, and this context creates our perception of the world.

Somewhere inside, we know our beliefs are not necessarily true, but they represent safety and predictability. We want predictability, even at the expense of truth.

Most beliefs are at least partly incorrect, and many are without basis. The good news is that we know they can change.

We've explored some of the ways we reinforce our beliefs and interpret everything that goes on around us through a lens that gives incontrovertible proof of the correctness of the belief.

Changing your beliefs so you can rebuild the world the way you want is the opportunity you hold in your hands if you dare to do it.

Going down the road of changing beliefs is not a journey for the timid. It is not easy to do and may bring consequences to you and others.

Sometimes it's important to drop a belief and adopt a new one regardless of the consequence. For example, there are cultural norms in some societies where cruelty to a specific group of people is ok. That has no place in our modern world.

Are there beliefs you've held that are so damaging that they must change without regard to what the collateral fallout might be? How did you deal with that change?

Most changes in beliefs are not so catastrophic, but instead, involve a substantial internal change that will dramatically affect you and the way you perceive and enjoy your life.

Even though most context changes are internal and significantly affect your attitudes and actions, they may also bring external reactions and consequences.

Let's look at the risks:

- Changing a belief that "you are responsible for others" may mean you no longer facilitate actions and circumstances that have served others but not you. This change may bring objection and rebellion from those who were the beneficiaries.

- Changing a belief that "you are inadequate" may mean that you spread your wings and begin to express yourself creatively. A negative reaction may come from those who have taken advantage of your creativity or generosity in the past.

- Changing the belief that "you are not capable of creating money" may put you on a path to wealth and independence that offends family or others who hold a different view.

- Changing a belief that "you are not that important" may

mean that you start to love yourself in a way that prevents others from taking advantage of you. That will meet with some opposition and resistance.

- Changing a belief that "you are not valuable and attractive" may mean that you attract attention and create success that others find envious. You may lose friends and create enemies.

- Changing beliefs, especially key ones, will set you on an entirely different path towards realizing the real capability and value of your soul. Those not prepared for this might object, withdraw support, ridicule or otherwise abandon you.

If your goal is to get through life without controversy while trying to please everyone, then changing deeply held beliefs from family, religion, or culture is a risky business.

As you embark on this journey and decide there is more available to you and that you are going to get it, do not interpret these adverse reactions as a sign that you are doing the wrong thing.

Anyone who expresses negativity as you grow is showing their jealousy, lack of capacity, or misunderstanding. It has nothing to do with who you are and what you can accomplish.

You were created with a purpose. As you discover and enjoy the growth that comes with expressing that purpose and creativity, your ability to ignore these adverse reactions will increase.

As you change and grow, it will not be your responsibility to convince others that you're on the right path. You have the right and the responsibility to form your own beliefs and context, and change by your intuition and connection with the Divine.

Chapter 8

THE REWARDS OF CHANGING BELIEFS

I am not suggesting that everything we believe is wrong or that all our experiences from parents, society, education, religion, socialization, culture, and other influences are somehow suspect.

We've been weaving a context from beliefs and living in the world with precisely these influences for millennia, and somehow, we have managed to get through it all.

What I am loudly proclaiming is this: if you have the feeling that something is missing or is not as it should be, then trust your intuition and carefully and thoroughly explore what the barriers are to achieving what you want.

We hear over and over, "you can have anything you want." The notion of creating life precisely as you wish it to be is bandied about regularly in self-help books and personal development courses everywhere.

My experience as a coach is that every client I've worked with is living far below their potential for creativity, expression, and fulfillment.

Because I practice what I preach, I regularly discover new layers of productivity, new fountains of creativity, and new sources of power in myself, which have been untapped.

Since the beliefs we have shaped every perception of our eyes and ears and every facet of the experience, it's life-changing when we realize that the filters we wear may be inaccurate.

These filters form the context with which we live.

I lived with the "absolute certainty" that I was "not good enough." It turned out to be a false belief. When I discarded it, I began to tap into creativity, influence, and opportunity I had scarcely imagined.

One fantastic example is in volunteer music work I have done in the church and community. Often in volunteer choirs, people are enthusiastic but doubtful of their skills.

By helping change the context, a little at a time, I've repeatedly seen a band of "ragtag volunteers," with widely varying levels of confidence and experience, turn into a great performing group, because they discarded the belief that they could not sing.

I have a client who changed from a frightened person with doubts about their worth to a powerhouse in negotiation that demanded and received significant compensation, all because they chose to change a belief.

I have another client who did not believe they had anything valuable to say. We worked together to change that belief. They went on to write a bestselling book and create an income opportunity that far exceeded the old imagined limit.

The most important benefit that comes from changed beliefs is not a significant increase in cash, a new job, or some other recognition from outside.

The most significant benefit is the change in how you view yourself and your ability to contribute to your world, just the way you want to.

You are a divine being with gifts and talents, sent here to do something meaningful. **When you come to believe you have that opportunity and the talent to make it real, everything shifts.**

You find new sources of confidence. You find the will and power to create your life precisely as you wish it to be.

You find the strength and insight on how to change circumstances that are harmful or holding you back from your opportunities.

You suddenly discover the freedom that comes from realizing that you don't have to "settle" for what you have now, or what is obvious.

You have the glorious privilege, opportunity, and even obligation to grow and contribute in ways that you can't see now but become evident as you go down this path.

The greatest benefit from examining and changing beliefs that are not true, even if they are tightly held and woven into the fabric of your DNA, is becoming the best version of yourself.

You then know who you are, why you are here, and what you are meant to do. You also have the courage and power to make it happen.

Chapter 9

VICTIM vs. OWNER: ARE YOU WILLING TO MAKE IT HAPPEN?

Despite the opportunity that lays before you; the truth is, most people don't dare to walk this road.

Something about the process is too frightening or too daunting to jump on this wild horse and ride it to the finish line.

You've heard the "victim" stories. They are only too predictable and typical. Likely you've used them at some time yourself. I know I have.

When things don't go the way you want, or life takes a sharp turn, it's easy to blame circumstances or others' actions for the mess.

There are times when circumstances are unfortunate, and things you try turn out poorly. Sometimes people make decisions or take actions that are exactly the opposite of what you thought they would do or what you think they "should" do.

That is how life works. What matters is what you do next. If you have a belief that you are stuck and have no options besides what you got served, you forfeit your right to grow.

Taking matters into your own hands and looking for the gift

in adversity is a skill that lets you rise above every circumstance. Perhaps not immediately and maybe not without considerable effort, but you can rise above the event.

Retreating to the victim's corner is a refuge that is always available to you. There you can lick your wounds, blame everyone and everything, and pretend that you have no control.

Feeling defeated, hurt, or disappointed is part of the glorious fabric of life. The choice you have is how long you choose to stay in that corner.

The language of a victim says, "look what they did to me." The language of the owner says, "what can I learn from this experience, and where do I go from here?"

A fundamental belief you must examine is whether or not you choose to be the victim of circumstance, others' behavior, and the vagaries of life.

Those who choose victimhood are those who settle for the easy and obvious and move through life complaining most of the time. Even when things go well, they don't know how to be grateful.

If you want to create the life you imagine, then start by adopting the owners' mindset as a definite first step. Understand that you own your life.

You are entirely responsible for every experience that you have in life. This doesn't mean that you can control every circumstance or others' attitudes and actions.

How you *experience* the events that unfold and what *you allow them to do* to your consciousness and your heart is absolutely under your control.

I like the word **fierce.** When you combine it with ownership, the idea of "fierce ownership" implies that you fully, and aggressively accept responsibility for creating your life. When you understand how precious this power is, hang onto it for dear life.

With this view, under no circumstance would you relinquish your ability to choose who you are, what you stand for, and what you will and won't do. This includes your ability to choose a reaction to every circumstance.

As an owner, you vigorously challenge every limitation that shows up in your world. You make a conscious choice about whether it's a barrier, and if you can live with this barrier.

You don't waste time challenging limits that are appropriate and give shape and meaning to your existence in a way that is uplifting and powerful.

At the same time, you don't waste any time *failing* to challenge boundaries that are inappropriate and don't allow you to contribute creatively to the people and circumstances around you.

As the owner of gifts and talents, you exercise your divine right of choice and ownership by examining and changing beliefs that no longer serve you and keep you from helping others.

Your willingness and ability to exercise fierce ownership of your life will be the source of great joy to you, exceptional service to others, and a meaningful contribution to your slice of the world.

"Choose to make today glorious.

Choose to make today outrageous.

Choose to give love.

Choose to be in integrity."

– Kellan Fluckiger

LEARNING TO IDENTIFY AND REPLACE BELIEFS

If it were as simple as saying, "Okay, I understand that beliefs are my creation and that I can replace them, so let's just get this over with," then we would be done.

The beliefs that you have came with time and reinforcement. They did not just show up one day and take over your mind.

The process of identifying and replacing the beliefs and context you have with something more correct and more aligned with whom you choose to be in the world also comes with time and reinforcement.

This section lays out a process to identify and then change the beliefs you have and the context by which you live. Like any process, it takes time and practice.

One of the big fallacies in all personal development work is that we imagine that because we "read the book," or "saw the YouTube video," then we have mastered a principle. This is not true and represents a big trap.

No one would imagine that because you watch 100 videos of the world's greatest tennis champion crush their opponents, you would somehow be a master at tennis.

Reading countless books on the techniques of the great chess masters do not qualify you to enter even the most rudimentary tournament.

We intuitively understand that all these skills take diligent practice. We do things and fail; we do things and get better; eventually, we do things and can demonstrate a level of proficiency.

All aspects of personal development are precisely the same. No progress takes place without all the requisite failure, gradual improvement, and eventual mastery.

The most significant impediment to learning is impatience, unrealistic expectations, and imagining that somehow, there is a magic wand to grant you a skill.

Take the time to learn the process. Determine in your mind that you will practice it until you get good at it. This unlocks the door and makes it possible for you to create precisely the life you want.

Chapter 10

CHOICES - WE HAVE THEM

The fact that we have choices is evident. If you go to the store to buy a pair of jeans, you have multiple options of style, fabric, color, cut, and fit.

We have choices about our cell phone provider and in some areas, options about who sells us electricity, natural gas or other services. We accept these facts as a matter of course, in modern life.

Somehow when it comes to our own lives, we build a world where we accept the false statement, "I had no choice."

That is utter nonsense. Nonetheless, we choose to accept it without question. What's going on here? It is a sad reflection of a collective and universal cop-out: "I won't challenge you if you don't challenge me."

When someone says, "I had no choice," what they often mean is that choosing one of the options produces an "obviously unacceptable outcome." There is subtle disempowerment there.

For example, the boss at work gives you a project to do with a deadline that means you'll have to work late every night this week and the weekend to have it ready by Monday morning.

You complain bitterly about the assignment and the requirements.

Your spouse asks, "Why didn't you just say no?"

You roll your eyes and say, "I had no choice." The implicit part of the conversation is that you assume that turning down the assignment would result in unfavorable treatment at work, or at worst, losing your job.

The truth is, you likely didn't talk to the boss about your other responsibilities, negotiate a different deadline, or do anything to explore other options. Perhaps you had tried before and decided now it was futile.

Even if you did, and there was no recourse or relief provided from that conversation, you still had the choice of accepting the assignment and its requirements or turning it down and perhaps leaving that employment.

You then make up all kinds of stories about why *that* choice is entirely off the table and impossible in your situation. The truth is, there are other options, and you could do something about it, but you don't want to.

You have every right to choose to accept the assignment. By taking the viewpoint that you had no choice and then accepting the assignment with frustration and resentment, you are damaging every part of the transaction.

Very likely, you will cut corners and do as little as possible to complete the assignment. You certainly won't bring your full effort and creativity to it.

Thus, the project suffers, and your position at work will probably suffer because what you turn in is not your best work.

You carry around negative emotions because you didn't want to do the assignment with its attendant schedule in the first place. You then live in a state of resentment and negativity for the rest of the week.

Perhaps you even carry it over to the next week and the one

after that. Maybe it colors your relationship with your supervisor for months or years to come.

You don't have a truthful conversation with your spouse about what your real options were or discuss what you did or didn't negotiate with your supervisor for a different schedule.

The potential consequence there is that your spouse feels neglected and believes you don't care that you are gone every night for a week and screw up the plans for the weekend.

If you decide to accept the assignment, keep the employment situation you have, and follow the given schedule, you have another choice.

You could go all in, do your best and blow your supervisor's mind with the excellence and thoroughness of your effort.

You could negotiate a deal with your spouse where you will reserve a weekend to do something special to make up for the lost time.

There are many other options I haven't listed. At a minimum, it's clear that you have many unexplored choices at every juncture in this circumstance.

I realize that I wrote this script and painted a particular scenario where I picked the choices and outcomes at every decision point.

However, I have seen this circumstance or something similar play out many times, with all the attendant consequences and negative emotions. It brings with it the hell of helplessness that comes from choosing to live in the victim's corner.

Why would you live that way? Is it a Habit? Belief? Context?

The first step in learning this process is understanding and acknowledging the choices that you have. Acknowledge them. Make them intentionally at each stage. Choose your attitudes and actions consciously to create the most potent outcome possible.

Chapter 11
THE PAST DOES NOT LIMIT YOU

One powerful constraint we fail to acknowledge and understand is that we allow our experience to limit the range of options we consider as possible.

We believe that what is possible is only what we've achieved. What was difficult will be difficult again. Negative people will still be negative. If we failed before, we would fail again.

This becomes self-fulfilling, and we spin around like a rat on a wheel.

The truth is that the past is only good for two things:

1. We start today, where we ended yesterday. For example, if you are traveling and you ended up in Denver, you begin the next day from Denver.

Wherever you left the project at work when you went home, that's where it will be in the morning.

This is even true with emotional issues. The passage of time blunts the neurochemistry of emotion, but unless you do some internal work or process some feelings from one day to the next, you will start your emotional circumstance the next day right where you left off.

2. The second thing the past gives us is lessons – if we choose to learn. By understanding the outcomes and consequences

of our attitudes and actions, valuable insight is available.

Accepting the idea that the future is always unwritten gives us the freedom to think about opportunities that are invisible when the past constrains our view. This is like driving a car with only a rear-view mirror.

Let us return to our example at the office. Suppose your supervisor has a pattern of callous disregard for the demands work puts on your personal life. Repeated conversation with the boss about this situation does nothing whenever a deadline looms.

Let us further assume that you have open and regular conversations with your spouse about the strain this puts on your relationship, your participation in your children's activities and other personal pursuits.

Even though you have given in to unreasonable demands and repeatedly accepted the undesirable requirements in the past (maybe you thought you'd gain favor with the boss), you're still in a position to make a different decision about the future.

You could elect to have a conversation with your spouse about leaving the company and plunging into the unknown of finding a new job, starting a business, or becoming a freelancer.

The lesson you learned from the past is that despite your willingness to repeatedly inconvenience yourself, there's been no recognition, no promotion, or special consideration at work.

You rightfully assume and expect that this trend will continue since there is no indication of any change in the works.

After careful consideration of what the past has taught you and recognizing the challenges that lay ahead, you decide that the unknown path is preferable to staying in a rut.

To do this, you have to discard a belief. Specifically, reject the belief that your current job is the best that you're going to find and that you are "stuck" in this circumstance.

Intellectually you may have realized that you were not stuck each of the previous times this happened. However, something about this present situation tipped the balance, and you chose to change your belief and to replace it with the belief that a greater opportunity lay around the corner.

This is a simplistic but relevant example of how we can either let the past dictate our beliefs or intentionally change the context and make a new decision.

Other substantial and consequential decisions that fall into this category might include:

- Changing the relationship between you and family members who are negative.

- Changing habits in your life that don't serve you.

- Changing careers entirely because you see industry trends that are concerning.

- Improving your health habits to lose weight or get in shape.

- The list goes on and on.

The critical learning here is that you're *not* constrained by what you think you know or have experienced in the past.

Past experiences have indeed created a set of beliefs. They may or may not serve you today. It is your opportunity and obligation to examine these beliefs and change them as appropriate so that you can create your life more powerfully.

Chapter 12

UNDERSTANDING AND OWNING
THE DEPTH OF CHOICE

In the previous chapters, we talked about a common and obvious choice about employment that you might face. Let's now explore other areas where we sometimes default to the victim's corner and say, "I had no choice."

One of the most obvious that has far-reaching consequences is our choices about relationships. These are weighty and vital choices with long-lasting effects.

When you get married or enter into a similar domestic contract, serious obligations come as part of this decision. Rather than continuing to take responsibility, I often hear people answering questions about relationships that default to the usual response, "I have no choice."

You always have a choice.

You had a choice when you got married. You chose that person and exchanged some promises, either the traditional way or vows that you wrote yourself.

Every day of your life, you elect *with a fresh choice* to remain in that relationship. This is far more than an intellectual exercise. You choose. It is victim speak to pretend otherwise.

The attitude of the choice determines how effective the

outcome is. You know that you could end the relationship and go away. Instead, you choose to remain.

When you default to the "I have no choice," attitude, what you are saying is that you have become lethargic and apathetic about the commitment and choice you once made.

It effectively says, the consequences of choosing to end the relationship are so drastic (or I imagine them to be), that I would rather stay in the situation that I'm in. Apathetic acquiescence is no way to create a robust future.

This is a perfect example of a belief, setting limits that don't exist.

If the relationship is important to you, instead of defaulting to continuing an apathetic commitment, acknowledge your fresh choice every day and every hour to remain in the relationship. Intentionally and vigorously staying faithful to your promises is a far more powerful position than merely settling for the status quo.

I cannot overstate the importance of this distinction. Staying with a previous decision by pretending you have no choice is weak and often leads to dissatisfaction. From the default stance, you live life settling for what is given instead of what you create.

Realizing that you have a choice and that you are free to renew your choice every hour and every day, puts a perspective in place that lets you live a more powerful life, fully committed to the marriage and your partner.

Choosing to treat the situation as if you had no choice creates a phony limit. It creates a perception of limited freedom, which leads to resentment.

This same distinction applies to every role that you have adopted in life. As an employee, you can leave at any time. As a parent, you can abandon those responsibilities without notice.

Each of these decisions brings with it a set of consequences that may or may not be acceptable to you. Establishing a pattern of ignoring the choices you have disempowers you and indicates a habit of refusing to take responsibility for the options you have in the present.

This shows up as a loss of energy, a loss of creativity, and a loss of interest in life. You lose the drive to grow and ultimately live life with blinders on because you have chosen to accept limits that don't exist.

Real freedom comes from recognizing the choices you have about what you do every moment, even if that choice is to repeatedly affirm decisions made earlier in life or earlier that day.

Powerfully accepting that choice and then throwing yourself "all in" to the consequences enhances your ability to create, live intensely, and build the life you want.

Chapter 13

STEP 1
WHAT DO I BELIEVE?

The next five chapters are devoted explicitly to the process required to identify and evaluate beliefs, make new choices, and apply those new beliefs to create a new context and a new life.

This process may sound simple, but it requires serious work. The fundamental attributes required are:

Honesty – You must tell the truth.

Openness – A willingness to explore new truths.

Courage – You must make some changes.

Commitment – You must stick with it.

Every day we come up against situations where we are torn between different decisions. They might be simple, like whether or not to put cheese on your hamburger or a recurring decision like whether or not to get up when your alarm goes off or hit the snooze button five times.

It might be something tough like whether or not to have a hard conversation about a situation that has been bothering you for a while, yet you keep putting it off.

Since we're talking about changing beliefs, simple things like what color T-shirt to wear or whether or not to have a cheeseburger don't rise to the level of a context discussion.

However, how you start your day does rise to that level. Certainly, the difficult situations that affect relationships or your work or your future also qualify.

The first step is to identify your current beliefs. The simple question is, "What do I believe about _____?" You fill in this blank. In the case of the alarm clock, you might say to yourself, "What do I believe about getting up when the alarm goes off versus hitting the snooze button a few times?"

The answer might be:

- I can skip taking a shower.

- It doesn't matter that much.

- I don't need to exercise.

- I can take a shortcut to work.

- Nobody will notice if I'm a little bit late.

- I can get my spouse to drop the kids off at school.

- I am exhausted, and I need to sleep.

- And 100 other answers.

The fundamental similarity in all these answers is that you will cut something out of your life that you had planned to do or are committed to doing to accommodate the sleep.

It also means you believe that whatever problem your snooze decision creates for someone else either doesn't matter, or you can brush it off and excuse yourself.

It also means that fundamentally, you don't care about keeping commitments to yourself. You believe that those little commitments, like what time you get up in the morning, don't matter.

It may sound harsh to describe it this way. That's why one of the essential ingredients is telling the truth about your beliefs.

Let's do the example of putting off the awkward conversation. "What do I believe about having a difficult conversation versus not having it?"

- I'm scared I'll be rejected.

- It doesn't matter anyway.

- It's none of my business, so I should keep quiet.

- Somebody's going to get in trouble.

- Maybe I'm wrong.

- Tempers will flare, and someone will be mad.

- Someone will be hurt.

- And many other things.

The common theme in all these is that the consequences of having the conversation will be worse for me than if I had kept silent, leaving things unspoken, and knowing they should've been handled.

Fear is creating a barrier that prevents the resolution of something that is out of order, which may have been festering for a long time.

The truth is that you don't know what will happen in any given situation. You don't know what anyone else is thinking, and the entire drama is taking place in your mind.

You've played both parts on both sides and pretended that you know outcomes you can't possibly be aware of.

The other truth is that if the situation is important, *it doesn't matter* what the other party may do. It's your opportunity to resolve the problem, and you keep avoiding it.

The critical point is to be brutally honest about what you believe about the situation, and not cover it up with any pretenses or hopeful thoughts.

Without exception, everyone that does this exercise is shocked, and often amazed at how frequently and how deeply the fear and negativity runs when they list true beliefs. This fear and doubt is manifest as hesitation or insecurity about a course of action.

This negativity and fear are invisible limits that are as effective as steel walls in keeping you from taking action that would be beneficial – a move that would either resolve the situation or provide clarity about further action.

As an initial assignment, I ask my clients to take the week between coaching calls, and during each day to be conscious of feelings. Whenever they feel any anxiety, stop to assess and write down their beliefs about the situation that is causing whatever they're feeling.

Whatever you identify as a limit you no longer accept, start with this question. "What do I believe?

It will take time and practice to get good at identifying your beliefs. It will take courage and honesty to list them clearly and truthfully.

If you have lived a life of unfulfilled expectations and unmet goals, this can be a challenging exercise. It is worth time and attention. There is no growth without effort.

For example, if you decide to go to the gym and set a goal to be able to do exercises at three times the weight you currently use, you must expect to go through a rigorous training program of some length.

Personal development and the ability to create a future you dream about is no different. There are no silver bullets and no magic wands.

The good news is that it gets easier with time and practice. You begin to realize that identifying beliefs that come from fear or uncertainty or past failures don't change the reality of the present.

This starts to create a sense of liberation as you realize all this is firmly in the past. You can leave it there.

The future is and remains unwritten. It's open for you to create any way you want.

Chapter 14

STEP 2
WHAT ELSE COULD I BELIEVE?

This next step requires exercising creativity and courage.

The degree of creativity and courage will depend on how powerful the existing belief is, how long you've held it, and the consequences that come from change. An example will illustrate.

Imagine you are a person who has an aversion to new foods. Somehow you've acquired the belief that food you haven't tried before, especially ethnic cuisine, will likely repulse you and taste bad.

How you came by this belief doesn't matter. Something about your experience has made you accept this as truth, and, consequently, you rarely try new food.

In applying step one, the current beliefs you might list are:

• This food will probably taste bad.

• New food always tastes terrible.

• I might throw up like I did that other time.

• And on and on.

Next, ask yourself, "What could I believe?" In a situation like this where the threat to you is relatively minor, you could list such possibilities as:

- If I take a tiny bite, it won't kill me.

- It doesn't look like it's all that bad.

- My friend ate some, and she liked it, so maybe it's okay.

In a low danger situation, it is easy to see how you might convince yourself to try something by changing the belief even slightly from "it will be bad," to "it might be okay."

That simple change in belief allows you to taste something new. This gives you further information for you to make a concrete decision based on the experience you have, instead of based on a limit that you created.

This situation frequently happens when we introduce people to new situations. Getting used to a domestic animal is one example where fear might be the first reaction, and then some degree of experience causes complete change.

Meeting a new person, getting a new job, or moving to a new place are other situations that often trigger resistance because of a belief that it will be uncomfortable and perhaps dangerous to your self-esteem.

A slight shift in belief from "I know this will suck," to "it might work out okay," is often all that is needed to give something new to try and then learn by experience.

I know that these are easy and obvious situations. I'm intentionally starting there to teach the principles because they are less threatening. The real power comes when you choose to tackle things that are standing in the way of your happiness, prosperity, and success.

There are two parts to answering the question, "What else could I believe?" The first part is the ability to articulate other possibilities. The second part is to hold the thought long enough to give life to the new belief or at least take action to experiment with the new idea.

In a situation with immediate action and consequences like tasting new food, you only have to hold the new thought long enough to pick up the fork and take the plunge.

When working with deeply emotional situations or beliefs that have been held for a long time, then both parts of this step becomes very difficult.

For example, if you hold a belief that you are not valuable or somehow "Not good enough," it may be difficult to articulate words to answer the question, "What else could I believe?"

If you can frame an answer and say something like "Well, I could believe that I might be good enough to make this happen," a host of opposition voices immediately launch in your head arguing the contrary position.

Every circumstance in the past where you have failed, or imagine that you have failed will be paraded before your eyes, and the internal critic launches a litany of trolling comments ripping your fledgling new thought to shreds.

The minute you create any new belief, it's attacked by the emotional memory of past experiences that have built and continually reinforce the "truth" of your inadequacy.

This encapsulates the difficulty of changing beliefs.

To combat this emotional onslaught, frame the question differently.

Sometimes we hear the question this way: "What could I believe and accept as a true possibility and say out loud without being embarrassed or laughing at myself?"

Answer this question instead: "What could I believe, (not saying that I do or that I think it's true,) or maybe (if I set all that noise aside and don't HAVE TO believe it right now,) accept as a possibility for a minute?"

In other words, step outside of yourself and the framework

of what you *think* you know and play with the question "What could I believe if nothing were in the way and I had no evidence to the contrary?"

You may need to practice learning to play with the question. Set aside all the negative voices of the past that rush in when you try to make this new possibility an actual belief.

Like everything, practice improves your skills. You will soon find that you can make a list of substitute beliefs without the sky falling or the world coming to an end around you.

The next part involves holding the thought about the new possible belief long enough to move on to the next question.

As long as the new belief stays in the "this isn't me" category, the thought is not threatening to your existing beliefs and context. The minute you try to move it into the category of real life, it then becomes a threat to your existing "knowledge." So don't do that, yet.

Leave it in the "not really" category. Treat it as a declaration of a state to come, for the time being. Then move on to the next steps.

When you are working on a longstanding belief, you already know all the reasons you have, and all the proof that you think demonstrates the validity of your old context.

To learn to hold the thought or fledgling belief long enough to be useful, we need to examine the "evidence" that you have amassed that seems to prove that the new belief can't be true.

The first thing to notice is that all that evidence comes from the past. Remember, in Chapter 3, "Where Beliefs Come From," all those fears and memories came from your rearview mirror.

Experience as a kid, involvement in school, failures or perceived failures in work or relationships or life or making money or whatever else the topic might be. All these so-called pieces of evidence are from the past.

In considering this "evidence," we must remember three essential truths:

1. We remember things much worse than they were. If someone else were to describe the very same situation we remember, their description would be nowhere near as big a disaster as we recall.

2. We often exaggerate the potential consequences of violating a piece of our context. A perfect example is the fear of public speaking. The truth is, regardless of the stage performance, the worst that can happen is an embarrassment. Left unexamined, that fear seems as big as death itself.

3. Even if the memory is entirely accurate, the future *is not an extension of the past*. Only if we insist on doing the same things as we did before is the same outcome likely.

This is where working with a coach is extremely valuable. Having a second set of eyes and an outside opinion as we talk about how our experience affects our current attitude, makes it is easier to see the truth and not be clouded by emotional judgment.

One natural parallel is in sports. As an athlete develops in their sport, they regularly come up against beliefs that they've reached the limit of their performance.

Becoming familiar with others who've smashed the looming barrier, working with a coach to understand what's required to improve and creating a context of possibility beyond their current score or record allows a person to reach new heights.

Countless world records have been shattered, and personal bests delivered, starting with changing the belief of "I can't do better" to "What if I can?"

Coming to the place where *you know* that you can create a

different future than your past is the key to allowing a new belief to take root.

What barriers are holding you in place and constraining your development? What beliefs about income, talent development, performance, or influence are keeping you chained to an imaginary block of concrete?

Starting in small ways will give you a track record of success, moving to a new belief. You can then leverage this success into confidence for more difficult areas.

Step two is to answer the question, "What else *could* I believe?" Do whatever is necessary to allow the possibility of a different belief to take root in your heart. A belief that may be more accurate, more authentic and indeed more useful to you than the current context you hold that limits your current performance.

Chapter 15

STEP 3
WITH A NEW BELIEF WHAT
ASSUMPTIONS FLOW?

Assumptions are the imagined consequences that you picture if you violate one of the beliefs that form your existing context.

We've all heard the story of the circus elephant who was trained at a young age with a chain and a stake in the ground.

The young elephant couldn't move past the end of the chain because the stake holds the elephant in place. No matter how hard the elephant tugs, nothing happens, and she can't move.

Later, when the elephant was full-grown and could rip the stake out of the ground with one motion of her large leg, she doesn't move past the end of the chain length.

She is *not* a prisoner of the chain and the stake. She is a prisoner of the belief that she can't move the stake because it has always been so. She assumes that it's pointless to pull and tug because it won't make a difference.

You have assumptions about the consequences of violating your context. For example, if you speak or get out of your desk without permission in elementary school, you assume you will get punished, your parents called, and you will get in trouble at home.

So you don't violate that limit. Instead, you sit in class even if you have to go to the bathroom – urgently. Consequently, you pee on the floor because of the assumption about the limit. In this example, I speak from personal 3rd-grade experience.

With the belief that the earth was flat, the assumption was if you sail too far, you would fall off and die. So you don't go. With the belief that you will fail at something, the assumption is that you should save yourself from embarrassment and not even try.

After creating a new belief in Step Two and learning to hold it long enough to give it life, a new set of assumptions follows. For example, a new belief is: "I used to believe the world was flat, now I believe it may be round."

With the old belief, you wouldn't sail because you assume you would fall off. With the new belief, you believe a different result is possible. You might say: "Well, we could launch a voyage and carefully test this new hypothesis."

If we return to our simple example with ethnic food, your new belief might be, "All new food isn't awful; in fact, much of it is good."

The new assumption from that position would be, "It might be fun to try out something new once in a while, and I would expand my horizons and get rid of this silly old fear."

A more relevant example of personal development is the all too common mantra, "I'm not good enough; I know I will fail."

With the concrete barrier from absolute "knowledge," you will fail; you assume that trying would be at least a waste of time and, at worst, an embarrassment.

As a consequence, you don't try new things and remain limited by the belief you hold. You stay in your rut. You have no promotion, no success, and keep spinning around and around on the wheel.

A new belief could be: "With the right support and opportunity,

I might not fail." An assumption that would flow from that belief is: "It's worth the effort to try."

Do not move on to creating assumptions until the new belief has some roots, and you can at least consider the possibility that the new belief is more valid than the old.

If you move too quickly, the assumptions will be difficult to frame. They will sound more like empty affirmations that you know are bogus and feel hollow and frustrating.

Be patient and stay with the possibility of a new belief. Allow the new belief to exist and ignore all the noise in your head, screaming about what's happened before.

If you do that, then creating the set of assumptions about the consequences of accepting and acting on the new belief will be easy to make.

Chapter 16
STEP 4
WHAT WOULD I DO
DIFFERENTLY?

Your current beliefs create a context that limits your life and constrains what you attempt and what you accomplish. Becoming conscious of how they restrict you turns the key to freedom.

After you identify those beliefs, you explore making changes. Then you articulate a new belief that you might be willing to accept and work on it long enough that it seems like a real possibility for you.

Then you identify assumptions about potential outcomes that would come if the new belief were true.

At this point in the process, it starts to get exciting. You begin to feel free as you consider the real possibility that the old beliefs form a context that is nonsense, overly constraining and very likely incorrect.

The better you do Step Two, and the only way to get better is more practice, the more real the alternate beliefs feel and the more power they begin to have in your heart.

Making assumptions about what would happen if the new

beliefs were true, then becomes a liberating exercise that helps you paint a new context in living color.

Now it's time for action.

If you have lived with an old belief for a long time, you already know what you would and wouldn't do when tied to the old concrete wall.

This step is about declaring what action you would take if the *new* belief were true. It is not an exercise in fantasy and requires a great deal of honesty, just like Step One.

Let's consider a typical example. Fear of public speaking is the number one fear that people face. Some rate it as more fearful than facing death.

Dying of embarrassment on stage is a condition never documented in the history of modern medicine, so we know embarrassment won't kill you.

If the new belief you declare about public speaking is: "I believe I might be able to stand in front of a group and talk about the therapeutic effect of animals, do a good job and teach the audience something valuable."

The assumption that would flow from this new belief is: "It would be worth it to take the time and effort to research such a talk, prepare it carefully and then deliver it to my intended audience."

The action that you would take with this assumption is to say "yes" instead of "no" when asked to deliver a speech.

The next action would be to do the research, prepare a talk, deliver it to a friend a few times, give it in the mirror a few times and then ultimately stand in the spotlight and do the thing that had terrified you.

You now have multiple victories. You have the victory of overcoming the fear, you have the triumph of changing a long-held belief that limited you, and you now *know* that changing beliefs for your betterment is possible – because you've done it.

Remember that choosing *what* you would do if you *did* believe, is the easy part. Owning the vision of the new future gives you the creativity and courage to act on the steps you specify. The first few steps make subsequent steps clear. Small success leads to confidence and more significant victories.

As in every endeavor, bold, courageous, consistent action is the key to creating real change. No amount of wishful thinking, collecting pictures for vision boards, or watching videos will smash the barriers and create the progress you crave.

On the other hand, creating a new belief, endowing it with power in your mind, making new assumptions about what is possible, and then taking the necessary action can't be stopped.

You can learn first-hand the truth of the statement, "you can truly create any life you can imagine."

Chapter 17

LEARNING TO CREATE A NEW CONTEXT

In the previous chapters, we explored the steps required to create a new life in your unknown future – a life free from the slavery of the past and its limiting grip.

The big question that always comes up here is, "How do I weave a new context from new beliefs and give it the kind of power needed to energize my assumptions and fuel the relentless action required?"

Creating anything involves time, energy, and some process or steps. Creating a new context is no exception, and because the beliefs in your context are intangible, much of the process comes from the inner game of consciousness.

There are seven parts to this step. It is where the rubber meets the road, and the actual work of change gets done.

As difficult as Step Two might be, where you work to accept the fact that you really *can* believe something different than your well-established habit, the thing that takes the most time is the exercise of this new belief until it becomes firmly entrenched in your brain and body.

The seven steps are:

Openness, Meditation, Ritual, Study, Perseverance, Forgiveness, Fun.

Openness

Openness to the idea that change is possible, not just for others, but also in your own life, is foundational. It all starts here.

For our purposes, we will define "openness" as a willingness to set aside an old context and its fundamental beliefs, at least temporarily, and embrace the fact that the magnificent brain and body you have includes the ability to change old beliefs and create a new context going forward.

Accepting the idea that what you think you know and what you have done in the past isn't the only path is the first step to exploring and then accepting new ideas that fit your situation, attract you, and help you change.

You don't have to be entirely open to everything all at once, but there has to be a ray of openness to get started.

Even if the best you can do is desire openness or want the things I've said to be true, that's enough to get started.

If you start with "this probably won't work, I've tried it all before, and it may work for others, but I'm the one person in the world that this absolutely won't help," then you're in for a rough ride.

If, on the other hand, you say "I don't know how this will turn out. I hope with all my heart that it works for me and I am willing to suspend judgment and go all in to see how to make change happen in my life," you are starting in the right place.

Meditation

Meditation is the first and best tool for unlocking the secret of changing beliefs. I'm going to begin with some basics because people with all kinds of ideas and experience with meditation will read this.

Meditation is not necessarily a religious practice, although it's a part of many spiritual traditions. It's simply learning to be still – to sit quietly with yourself and set aside other distractions. Here is a definition we will use for this work.

Meditation is:

- Slowing the mind and body down enough to be where and when you are. I describe this as "Learning to be present."

- Quieting the mind long enough to see what is there.

- Trusting that what your intuition brings to you is the truth.

Slowing down the mind and body is a massive challenge for some. If your habit is to be on the go, physically or mentally, at all times, then this may seem impossible.

Start with physically slowing down. Sit quietly by yourself for 10 minutes. "Listen" to the silence, as best as you can, avoid fidgeting, avoid listening to noises or conversations in other rooms, or anything else that's a distraction.

It's easiest to do this if you find a quiet place where you won't be disturbed for 10 or 15 minutes — work on just quieting the body and being okay with the stillness.

Your mind may still be racing and frantically invaded with random thoughts during the entire time. We will work on that next, but for now, practice sitting still for 15 minutes until being physically still for this long doesn't present a challenge.

The next step is to repeat the quieting process with your mind.

However difficult it was to do with the body, it is exponentially harder with that massive computer on your shoulders.

The goal is not to empty your mind to nothingness, but to exercise your ability to direct your thinking. This is how you begin to be the master of your thoughts.

If you are in an office and you're on the phone, deeply absorbed in an important conversation, and someone knocks on the door or walks in, you do something about it.

Perhaps you wave them off. Maybe you excuse yourself on the phone and then quickly explain that you are busy, and the inadvertent intruder must come back later.

However you handle it, your determination to return to the important matter on the phone allows you to dispatch an interruption quickly.

Quieting the mind is much the same. Pick a single thought that will be the focus of your concentration. Some people start with the breath. Focus on what it feels like to breathe.

You can pick anything you like as your focus, as long as it's pleasant. You can use the face of a loved one or a favorite place that is peaceful and quiet such as a favorite vacation spot.

Whatever you choose – focus on it in a relaxed and pleasant way. Whenever intruding thoughts come, and they will set them gently aside and return to the thought that you've chosen as your focus.

If you want a beginner's guide that gives several different approaches to meditation, there are many sources available. One book is *Meditation; The Amazing Journey Within.*

I wrote that book several years ago to help those new to meditation get started quickly. I have more information about it in the appendix.

The good news is, you can't do it wrong. There are no mistakes and no need to feel like "I can't do this." Learning the skill of setting thoughts aside and returning to a focus is learning the practice of meditation.

The reason that meditation is the foundation skill is simple: as you change your context for life, old habits and beliefs will intrude with regularity and with annoying force.

Developing your ability to set these thoughts aside and return to the adjusted belief you have chosen is a critical skill in making a new belief permanent.

If you haven't practiced meditation before, start with a focal point that is something you enjoy. Do not start with a belief you are trying to change. Practicing with new beliefs at the same time you learn meditation is difficult for two reasons.

Learning to meditate is learning a new skill. This takes work and focus, even starting with an easy focus point like breathing or the face of a loved one. If you add to that the mental argument about accepting a new belief, it is much harder to learn.

It's easier to learn meditation, without the struggle of trying to use a thought that causes conflict as your focus point.

I cannot stress strongly enough the criticality of learning to meditate. If you want success, learning to meditate is not optional. It is the key to your mental and spiritual operating system.

Even with all the scientific research and evidence which demonstrates the power and benefits of meditation, I regularly have clients who try to bypass this piece, thinking it's unnecessary or weird.

There is no other way. Meditation allows you to access the operating system of your mind in a way that no other skill allows.

Also, there are a host of physical and spiritual benefits that come to the body by learning to meditate. Modern medical studies have extensively documented these benefits.

Besides all that, our focus here is to learn the skill of directing your thinking, so you are armed with the most powerful tool available, as you create new beliefs to replace old ones.

Practice your meditation every day, 15 minutes in the morning and 15 minutes at night. I promise you, without exception, it will be the best 30 minutes of your day.

At first, it may seem frustrating and pointless, but I guarantee that as you get better at it and getting better only comes with practice, it will be a refuge for you physically, emotionally, and spiritually.

As your skill with meditation improves, your ability to accept a new belief as at least a possibility will get easier and more natural.

Soon you will develop the skill to entertain the possibility of a new belief easily. Also, you will have developed the ability to set aside negative voices that attack you when you choose to change.

Once you begin the practice of meditation, commit yourself to form a lifelong habit. I am not overstating its importance by telling you it is the most powerful tool you have to create lasting and meaningful change in your life.

Ritual

Essentially, the beliefs you have are mental habits. They are the default operating system that guides you through every circumstance in life.

The difficulty of changing your context and its constituent beliefs depends directly on how deeply held the beliefs are and your degree of openness. The more profound and more fundamental you hold this belief, conscious or not, the more difficult it is to accept something new.

In physics, Work = Force x Time. The amount of work done

is equivalent to the force applied multiplied by the length of time that force is applied.

The strength of a belief can be represented the same way: Strength of Belief = Frequency of Reinforcement x Power of Signal.

A subtle message reinforced thousands of times, such as children received from their parents, creates beliefs of incredible depth and power.

Such a belief for me was "I am fundamentally flawed." This came from thousands of repeated negative messages and physical punishment that I received throughout my childhood.

On the other hand, an event that happens once, if it was traumatic enough, can also create a belief that is forceful and deeply entrenched.

An obvious example is a certainty you have that touching a hot heating element on a stove will burn your hand. One experience is enough.

Since most beliefs were formed slowly over time, changing these long-standing beliefs is going to require similar repetition.

For example, imagine that you are standing in the woods. On the left is a well-worn path that you have taken many times. That path represents a particular belief for you. It is some limiting truth that you have accepted as fundamental and unchangeable.

You have walked it thousands of times, and it is your natural reaction to a given circumstance. It is your habit. You don't even think about it, every time a specific stimulus or situation happens, there you go again.

You know by experience that it leads to the "pond of disappointment." The place where you are not satisfied with the outcome, not happy with yourself, and you longingly wish that you could do better or be like someone else.

You have heard about the "pond of success," and that it's somewhere to your right. You are not sure how to get there, and no path leads to this new destination from where you stand.

Perhaps you consult with someone who gives you directions to the "pond of success." They point you in a different direction through the woods. You look in that direction. It's covered with grass, thistles, overgrown bushes, and brambles.

You can't see the destination, and you wonder if they're wrong. You know if you go that direction you are going to get burs in your socks, scratches, and generally be in for a rough trek.

You make a courageous choice to follow the direction they pointed because you want something different for yourself. You bravely cut your way through the bushes, eliminating some of the branches and barriers between you and your intended destination.

You fight your way through and make it. Now you know it is there. You made it once. However, the next time you stand at the place of decision, the well-worn path to the left is smooth and inviting. After all, you have walked it thousands of times.

You now know where to go if you choose to go to the right, but the path is not well worn, and it is only slightly easier than last time.

The choice you have each time is whether to blast your way once again through the difficulties including some scratches and burs, or default to what is comfortable.

You know that if you take the hard way a second time, the path will be better marked and a bit easier than the first time. Still, as you stand at the fork, the decision feels hard.

The value of ritual is to prepare yourself every day by *deciding ahead of time* what you will do when faced with a decision and engaging in intentional actions that put you in a courageous frame of mind before you reach that decision point.

Let me be specific. Creating a "morning ritual," where you

contemplate and reaffirm your new belief and determine that you will maintain this context at all hazards, makes it easier when the choices come.

On the days you don't prepare yourself, if you are the least bit distracted or tired when you get the decision points, you will automatically default to the well-worn path and find yourself with the result that you know so well.

A complete morning ritual will prepare you spiritually, physically, emotionally, and mentally to make the choices and keep the commitments you have made to yourself.

Meditation is an essential part of that daily preparation ritual. Using that time to reinforce your belief in the choice before you reach important decision points puts you in a more powerful place when they come.

For example, a simple formula I use is to provide myself with one hour of preparation time every morning. I do this regardless of my schedule. I adjust the time I get up to accommodate this ritual.

This might sound extreme when you have early appointments, but if you go into your day without being fully prepared, you are guaranteed to perform at less than your best. Why would you do that when you are in the process of changing your beliefs and creating a better context for yourself?

At a minimum then, my daily morning ritual looks like this:

- Spiritual preparation – 15 minutes of meditation including the critical area of self-love.

- Physical preparation – 10 minutes yoga or other stretching.

- Emotional preparation – 10 minutes working on a relationship by sending a text or message to someone important to me.

- Mental preparation – 10 minutes reading a chapter in a stimulating book.

This is just an example, and I adjust the ritual regularly so that I prepare myself at this minimal level no matter what the schedule for the day is.

The difference in my energy and performance between the days I faithfully do my ritual and days I do not is stark and obvious.

It is vital that your ritual address all the parts of your life to be most effective. My choice to divide life into those four components (Spiritual, Physical, Emotional, and Mental) is founded on my own experience and experimentation. I also have many case studies from clients that validate the system.

How you create your ritual and what you do will be your individual choice. Experiment until you find something compelling that enables you to change beliefs more rapidly.

If you want more information or help in creating a ritual that works for you, please see the appendix at the end of the book for resources and contact information. Part of the work I do as a catalyst for change is to help clients identify and create a habit of a powerful ritual.

Study

As you become committed to the idea that you control your destiny and can change even your most fundamental beliefs, you will want to learn more.

There are hundreds of books and thousands of videos on YouTube and other Internet sites devoted to both the practice and the science of transformation.

Medical research, brain scans, psychology, and all the related disciplines are converging more and more powerfully on the idea that we decide our future based on our beliefs.

Take the time to find content that inspires and uplifts you and reinforces your desire to change and your commitment to stay with the process.

Listen to your chosen content as you walk the dog or drive to work or at any time. Each of these sources will have a slightly different take on how it works or how to go about it. Find what resonates with you and use it. If you want information on the material and programs I have, consult the appendix.

All of these resources represent the authors' personal experience and how they have made these personal development processes work for them. Don't let this diversity of conversation confuse or dissuade you.

Gathering information and hearing all this conversation is fantastic. Remember that watching 1000 videos will not change your fundamental beliefs about yourself, your limiting context or anything about your life, if watching the videos is all you do. If you want real change, you must go through the steps outlined above.

An example will illustrate. If I sign up for a gym membership and make a commitment to get strong enough to do 100 push-ups, the only way to get there is by doing push-ups.

Watching someone else do 100 push-ups and watching videos of incredible athletic feats will not make the change. It won't matter how many times I watch them or how many times I'm blown away by the efforts of others; only my work will bring about the change.

The ongoing study of the brain is exciting and demonstrates both the scientific frontiers and the personal experiences of those who are living the truth that beliefs can change and that we all can create our own lives.

These books, videos, conferences, and workshops can serve as instruction and motivation for you, but they will not do the work. I can't tell you how many times I have worked with clients who throw up their hands in frustration and wonder how come they are not further along in their progress.

I ask them how much effort they have put into the process, and the answer I get is that they regularly watch videos, go to conferences and read books.

The effort spent on the actual work is minimal. Instead, each time frustration sets in, they go to a new conference or listen to a new video. They want the shortcut. There isn't one. Only push-ups will make my arm stronger – my push-ups.

Perseverance

I have to keep at this until I succeed. If I crash my way through the forest and get to the "pond of success" once or twice, and then don't continue the process, the path to that destination will never become well-worn.

If I keep pounding my way through the forest to the new destination, eventually, that path becomes well-worn, and then it becomes the default path.

The old path is now overgrown with weeds and difficult to find. Now I wonder how I ever could have chosen that old direction in the first place.

Perseverance is not an accident. You will need to discover sources that rekindle your enthusiasm and commitment to adopt and then embrace the new beliefs and context in your life.

Accountability structures, hiring a coach, and revisiting the reason you want to make the change are three ways to keep the fire burning. There are many others. You will need to find and commit to those sources of inspiration that move you.

What I know from my personal experience and the experience of hundreds of clients, is that without the ritual, without continual recommitment to the new belief and without some tools to reinforce your perseverance, the power of the old belief will have you walking that familiar path before you realize what happened.

If you genuinely want to be the architect of your future and create precisely what you imagine, why would you spare any effort in putting together a process and getting the help that most likely will bring about your success?

Perseverance is a funny thing, ask any addict. Anyone who has tried to overcome an addiction, whether it is to a substance or a bad habit, knows exactly what I mean.

When you think you are clear and don't have to do the rituals that got you clean and keep you clean, you find yourself believing or behaving in a way exactly the opposite of what you committed to.

Remember that the habits and beliefs that are deeply entrenched formed over years or even decades of reinforcement.

My battle with "I am fundamentally flawed," came from decades of wading through Major Depressive Disorder (MDD) brought about my being abused as a child.

Perseverance is a blessing, not a chore. If you think of the word as a constant fight instead of a joyous choice, then it becomes much more difficult than it needs to be.

Remember that you are about creating changes in your life to have what you want. Maintaining that vision will help you when the old beliefs pull strongest.

Forgiveness

You may be wondering what forgiveness has to do with this whole topic. It is an essential element; without it, you guarantee failure.

No matter how many rituals you do and how many safeguards

you put in place, there will be times when you default to the old path, and the old habits and beliefs overwhelm.

When that happens, you have a choice. You can engage in an endless cycle of self-flagellation and loathing, or you can forgive yourself and move on.

A telltale sign is a client who asks me, "how come I'm the person that just can't seem to get this?" This is another label. They have labeled themselves as a permanent failure.

Failures, setbacks, struggles, steep hills to climb, and other barriers are all part of the growth process.

Think about what a tree goes through each year. Every year a tree adds a ring to its growth. You can tell the age of a tree by counting the growth rings.

You can also tell a lot about the weather by looking at the growth rings. In years of a lot of rain, the growth rings are wider, and in years of drought, the growth rings are so thin that they might barely be noticeable.

I planted an orange tree in my backyard in Phoenix. If you know anything about citrus, you know that citrus trees do not bear fruit the first year and perhaps two of their lives.

If I gave up and ripped it out after the first year, or if the tree gave up and said: "I'm useless, I can't even produce an orange," I would miss all the fruit of following years.

Instead, I left the tree alone, watered it, and waited. Sure enough, after a couple of years, it began to produce beautiful and succulent oranges. My ritual was watering the tree. The tree's ritual was the miracle that takes place that causes growth.

The outcome was a crop of oranges that were very tasty.

I noted in the beginning that changing beliefs, particularly fundamental ones that have been your barriers for a long time, is a process, not an event.

Every setback is a blessing, every bump in the road is a lesson, and every failure is an opportunity to take stock of what happened and learn from it.

Forgiveness is the act of not being hard on yourself and creating an additional barrier by adding emotional baggage to the process.

Forgiveness means learning from what happened and then move past it. Stay focused on the prize; love yourself more and move on.

If you are serious about accomplishing real change, you are on a journey that few undertake, and even fewer succeed. Most are content to live in mediocrity and accept what is in front of them.

Most are unwilling to go through the rigors of challenging their own beliefs and exploring what is possible. Who knows what can come by painting a masterpiece on the unwritten page of the future?

Fun

This section would not be complete without talking about fun. The process of personal development is not trivial. It is rigorous.

If you've ever climbed a steep mountain, you know what it means to walk a rigorous trail. However, when you get to the top, the view is lovely, and the sense of accomplishment is amazing.

When you talk about the climbing experience later, it is an adventure, complete with the story of aching thighs, thorns in your socks, and spills on slippery rocks.

However, the overall experience was a joyful one.

You are walking the road that many have walked before you. Your capability and divinity are just as robust as anyone else's. You can make this happen.

If you choose to have fun in the process, two things happen. First, it becomes easier because something fun is more attractive than something onerous. Second, it creates a better memory that is more attractive and will help you repeat the process.

We all have experience with going through something difficult while at the same time knowing that in a year from now we'll laugh about it.

This process works the same way. Challenging and rigorous at the time, but joyful and satisfying at the end.

It is easier to create fun if you don't make these changes in isolation. Whatever support system you need around you, build it. That support must be a high priority.

You might seek a trusted friend, a support group, a coach, or another mechanism. The more you can share about your process and progress, the easier it becomes, and the faster you get finished.

Choose to make it fun.

"If you choose to live in truth, the lens of your life becomes clearer, opportunities become obvious, and problems become solvable."

Kellan Fluckiger

PUTTING CONTEXT TO WORK

S ection 1 gave us the principles.

- You are living the life today that you create.
- You are constrained by the context you create from your beliefs.
- You can change your beliefs and your context.
- You can create any life you want to have.

Section 2 gave us the steps to changing beliefs and weaving a new context.

- Identify your current beliefs.
- Pick new beliefs.
- Create new assumptions and actions.
- Do the work to create a new context from the new beliefs.

Section 3 will give us practical tools and processes to make this work.

- Understand why we cling to the old.
- Use the power of habit to serve you.
- Use the power of Choosing, Declaration, Action, and Practice.
- Stick with it until you win.

If you want real success, you have to do the work that applies to your situation.

I will give you some specific examples, with as much detail as I can, without being personally acquainted with your situation.

My personal development work and the years of practice with clients have given me a rich tapestry from which to draw experience and examples.

If you go through this section carefully and honestly, you will be able to identify with the examples and see situations that are like your own. Then you can make this work for you, giving you both the courage to start and clear ideas about how to make it successful in your life.

Please get the help you need to make this work for you. Get a coach. There is no better or faster way to change your life in a big way than with a good coach.

If you read through this book and do not make a decision to start putting this powerful tool to work for you, then this will be one more of those books you read, and nothing will change.

The real value will come as you choose to tell the truth to yourself, make some serious commitments, and get to work.

Before we get to specifics let us review one more time what we already know:

1. You are limited by what you believe. Whether these beliefs come from history, culture, religion, family, personal experience, or other sources, these beliefs weave the context of concrete walls that limit what you have and what you will attempt.

2. Because you either accepted these beliefs or created them, these limits exist only in your mind and do not stop you from being or accomplishing something more.

3. If you accept this truth and take the appropriate steps,

your context will change, if you make a declaration, change your behavior, and stick with it.

4. There is no limit to what you can accomplish if you discard the barriers that arise from your beliefs, change your context, and never quit.

Let's get started.

Chapter 18
TRIGGERS

The first step in the personal application is to start recognizing situations where your context is artificially limiting your progress.

You will learn to identify these faster and spend less time in your jail and more time making progress.

Every person is different. Your situation will vary from what I describe, but there are commonalities that I have seen in my years of work in this area. Approach this with the intent to find ways to make it work instead of creating excuses why it won't

Regardless of your circumstance, habits control most of your life. You do many of the same things every day and every week. Studies suggest that 85 to 90% of our daily attitudes and activities are habit-based.

You drive the same way to work. You have the same conversations or at least conversations that are so close to identical that changing a few words still makes them sound like a broken record.

You visit the same people and engage in the same things week after week, month after month and year after year.

Habits make awesome servants but terrible masters. Many habits ingrained so deeply that they become part of our physiology and are repeated over and over again with zero thought whatsoever.

There is nothing wrong with this if a habit serves you. However, many habits are continued long past their usefulness and even past the point where we know that they have become damaging.

For example, you may be an avid coffee drinker. You have learned and perhaps been told by your physician that caffeine is causing you problems and that you should give it up.

The habit is so strong that the mental and physical addiction has you stopping at Starbucks without even realizing what you are doing. You tell yourself that one more day won't matter as you sip your double shot latte on the way to work.

We each have thousands of such habits. How do you know which practices are harmful, which beliefs are keeping you locked in prison and what piece of your context is serving as a ball and chain to your productivity and prosperity?

One telltale sign is a feeling of *resignation*. You want to do something, and the first thought you have when you consider this new thing is that you are stuck where you are.

A perfect example is changing jobs or changing careers. You say to yourself "I have always wanted to own my own business because I love repairing furniture."

The thought of doing such a thing frightens you a little but excites you at the same time. The overarching feeling, however, is one of resignation because when you consider all the reasons that this is not the right choice for you, you don't see a way to get started.

No one in your family was an entrepreneur. You know several people who have opened their own business and failed. You've been told that you have no aptitude for business. You believe you don't know where to start.

You have too many obligations, and you are not sure your spouse would support you. You dread the thought of actually cutting the cord to the "sure thing" of your job.

The endpoint of the conversation is that the daydream slips from your mind. The feeling of resignation in your stomach adds to the certainty that you will probably never make such a move. Back to the "maybe later" pile.

Let's look at the excuses. There are millions of entrepreneurs. There are vast resources of advice, books, coaches, classes and other help that you could have from people besides your family.

The fact that you knew several others who failed means nothing. Most businesses fail. You have no idea what steps they took to prepare or whether or not they got available help.

What difference does it make what other people tell you about your aptitude and capability? That is their belief and their context, why would you adopt it as yours?

No one automatically knows where to start. You do some research; you talk to successful entrepreneurs, you take a "starting your own business" class at a community college or Chamber of Commerce and then you know where to start.

Everyone has obligations. You will have them until you're dead, so a pile of responsibilities is no reason to avoid starting a business.

In conversations with your spouse, you have probably prefaced them with negative energy and filled them with your doubts. It would be no wonder that they would be skeptical and worried.

The job you have is no "sure thing" after all. Don't think for a minute that the company wouldn't fire you if it suited their purposes. There's no such thing as job security.

If you considered for a moment that all these answers to your doubts are *just as true or truer* than the imaginary barriers you have erected, it paints an entirely different picture.

Another telltale sign that you are living in a false context is *feeling stuck* or choosing to live in eternal yearning for something you can "never achieve."

An example of this would be an unfulfilled desire to change something dramatic in your personal life. Let's suppose a busy job, and a sedentary lifestyle has brought you fifty extra pounds.

You make excuses about why you can't play with the kids, you dropped out of the community basketball league, and your favorite television shows have suddenly become irresistible.

You have several relatives that are overweight, and many people in your office have suffered a similar fate. You all stand around and blame the demands of the job for your obesity.

You have the nagging feeling that something should be different. You know that others have lost weight but believe that it is beyond your reach. You don't have the time or energy that is necessary for the change.

You do not know where to start. You do not know where to get support. You think your doctor told you once you have a thyroid problem and so you are *permanently stuck*.

Without going through all the excuses like we did the first time, it is easy to see that these beliefs, though powerful, are just as phony as the last batch.

They are a context woven from beliefs *you choose to accept* and not challenge.

Every one of them has an answer and is subject to immediate change.

Six months from now you could be in shape, fit and coaching your kid's soccer team if you want to change your context and blow down the walls of your prison.

More examples of false barriers:

- Any time you are feeling wistful.

- Any time you feel overwhelmed.

- Any time you claim you are too old.

- Any time you say it's too late.

- Any time you feel powerless.

- Any time you hear the same excuses run through your mind or out of your mouth again and again.

- Any time you are blaming others or the government or the economy or God.

- And on and on and on...

These are all excellent indicators that you are stuck in a prison of context.

If you are ready to do battle and create the life you want, pick one. For starters, pick an easy one, to get a quick victory and so you don't go up against the formidable army of beliefs from habits entrenched in the very cells of your body.

Chapter 19

POWERFUL CHOICES

In Chapter 14 we addressed the question "What else could I believe?"

We discussed the difficulty of changing beliefs in our current context and the assault that comes from our old habits when we try.

In Chapters 10, 11 and 12 we learned that we do have choices that are not limited by the past and that every single person, including you, have these choices. You are not an exception to the truth that you can change your beliefs and change your context.

So how do you make great choices instead of wimpy wishes? Choices that carry the ring of authenticity and possibility, instead of wishful thinking that carries the seeds of automatic defeat?

The Value of Choosing

Step one is to make a choice. Many people spin around forever claiming a "lack of clarity" in deciding what they want to be different in their lives.

Unable to pinpoint with absolute precision an outcome before starting becomes a convenient excuse for eternal procrastination.

Every choice you make is temporary. It is a test. After you choose, if you get down the road and decide that the option isn't precisely lined up with what you want, adjustments can be made.

I guarantee that whatever you choose, you will make adjustments to have it continue to fit your desires as circumstances unfold.

It is rare to walk into a store, grab a suit off the rack, and have it fit exactly. It happened to me once. I walked into a secondhand store for designer clothes and took a Zegna suit off the rack.

It felt like it had been tailored for me. The fit of the jacket, the length of the pants, the color, everything was perfect. I was thrilled, and of course, I bought it instantly. But like I said, that's only happened once in my life.

Mostly, choices we make need fine-tuning. As you fashion new beliefs to weave a new context for your life, you will also make alterations.

The value is in the choosing. Making a choice stops the hesitation and dance of uncertainty, gives you a place to start and means that you have taken the first steps.

Your first belief changes will be tentative, fraught with resistance from your habits, and feel a bit uncertain. Make them anyway.

The Courage of Declaring

Step two is to declare the choice. Countless resolutions that seem like a good idea when you think of them fade quickly if they remain in the closet of your mind.

Declaring your new belief and the effect you expect it to have on your context and life is powerful. It is a tool that will strengthen your resolve and hold you accountable.

I know many who say they want to get in shape but won't make such a declaration to their family, colleagues at work, or anyone else.

Afraid they will fail, they are more tuned in to the embarrassment of starting and quitting than the suffering of staying out of shape and in the rut.

There is an awesome power that is mobilized in the act of declaring your new belief. You have to start somewhere. If you can't tell anyone immediately, go into the closet and stick your face in the clothes and scream your choice at the top of your lungs.

Then, write it down in a Facebook post, tell people in your family and at work. Make it part of the fabric of your day. Every day. After the initial declaration, tell these same people about your progress every day.

The old beliefs and context you have now only gained power with repetition over weeks, months, years, and perhaps decades.

If you are making changes, you want every single advantage you can have. Stack the deck in your favor. A bold declaration and constant repetition add to the power you need to combat the weight of old habits and beliefs you choose to change.

This takes courage. Exercising that courage is empowering and gives you an additional sense of control. As we described in chapter 18, one of the hallmarks of the limits imposed by your existing context is that you feel powerless.

When you exercise courage and make a strong declaration, you are reaching out to unalterably grab back your power and take control of your context and your life.

The Power of Action

After making a firm choice about your new belief and a clear declaration about your intention to make it true, comes the test of fire.

Nothing substitutes for action. Nothing gives you clarity and power like the first time you take steps on the course dictated by the new choice.

Hacking your way through the underbrush and reaching the pool of success for the first time is exhilarating like nothing else. Your body is exhausted, you have thistles in your socks and scratches on your face and arms, but all that vanishes as you move into the clearing and see what you have achieved.

For an action to be successful, it cannot be random and without adequate preparation. Depending on how long the habit or belief has been part of your context, the action to change it could be challenging and time- consuming.

To increase your odds of success, start with something easy. Think carefully about what must be different in your life to create success. Then go after it with gusto.

With clients who are committed to change, a natural place to begin is the creation of a powerful daily ritual like the one described earlier in the book. Use the four parts of life I described or create your own. Carry the intention to develop a more powerful version of yourself.

Often this will require a change in the alarm clock. Deciding to get up earlier can be difficult, but if the reward is an effective preparation for every day, then fulfilling the choice carries its own reinforcement.

What needs to be different for you to get up one hour earlier every day? Is there a television ritual that you have now that needs to be changed or eliminated?

Do you have an internet browsing habit that could be eliminated to make room for your new belief and context?

You might need to set two alarm clocks, one across the room that is loud and annoying, so you cannot ignore it. Perhaps you must put a third one, set five minutes later, in the bathroom, so you have no choice but to get at least that far.

What stories about getting up in the morning at a particular time do you need to eliminate? Perhaps you have told yourself, "I am a night person." That is just a story. Your body can be trained to adopt any schedule that you choose.

Creating a plan of action that supports your new belief and then adding accountability for that action is the most powerful way to begin the reinforcement of a new piece of context.

Chapter 20

PRACTICING EFFECTIVELY

I started teaching piano at age 17. My first student was a girl who was three years older than me. I was intimidated, and it was difficult for me to give her assignments.

My hesitation made my skill as an instructor less effective because I was scared to say everything I thought needed to be said.

Over the years, my confidence grew, and I learned many techniques and tips that increased the effectiveness of the lessons and the practice time spent by the students.

One such technique is "counting out loud." All music has a rhythm, and often that rhythm is marked by measures of three beats or four beats.

I learned that students that counted the rhythm "out loud" made far more progress in gaining rhythmic understanding and ability to sight read music than those that only counted by tapping their foot or saying the numbers in their minds.

Some students had real difficulty with this because it felt embarrassing. Those who merely followed directions had great success and advanced much quicker than those that didn't.

As you practice identifying old beliefs that form your current limiting context and then experiment with changing those limits by committing to and performing the required actions, you will see growth before your eyes.

If you practice effectively and consistently, you will create and perfect a skill that will benefit you forever. If you take shortcuts, you will get discouraged and quit.

There is an old saying, "practice makes perfect." This isn't true; a more accurate statement is, "perfect practice makes perfect." Since none of us are perfect, we need to direct our focus to make our practice as perfect as we can.

The first assignment I give clients to start changing context is to play a game. You can play along right now.

For the next seven days, stop what you are doing ten times during the day. Consciously step out of your normal thinking and routine into the "observer/chooser" mode where you are detached.

Choose each of the ten times by noting when you feel awkward, clumsy, uncertain, frightened, resigned, stuck, or any of the telltale feelings that let you know you've hit an imaginary wall.

Take a piece of paper and jot down the beliefs you have about the current situation. Be truthful and describe the context of that situation.

Objectively think about the reason for the barrier. What are the beliefs that you listed that cause you to accept the barrier as a final limitation?

After you have written down the beliefs that comprise your context, go through the exercise of choosing a new belief that is more empowering and more truthful.

Start with something small and with changing one belief at a time. This prevents the exercise from becoming overwhelming and creating discouragement.

Go all the way through until you pick a new belief, identify the assumptions that flow from that new belief, and select a different course of action.

This may seem like it will take a long time, but once you start doing it and get used to telling the truth right away, it becomes fun and empowering.

Experiment with the actions you would take following establishing a new belief. Make a note about the outcome that follows the new choice of action.

Give yourself the gift of doing the complete exercise. If you forget to do it ten times, then do it nine times. If you forget to do it nine times, do it as many times as you remember.

The point is to start, experiment, adjust, and then repeat. Don't skip any steps. I get asked all the time if it is "really necessary" to write down the beliefs that form your context.

The answer is simple; it is only necessary if you want the exercise to be as powerful as it can be. Listing the beliefs only in your mind carries a fraction of the power that writing them down does.

When you write down your beliefs and look at them as a whole, it's easy to see how they form the context of what you feel and how you act in a given situation. Seeing it on paper in black and white carries a powerful message about how you are creating barriers in your life.

As I go through this exercise, I am often shocked as I look at my list of beliefs. I write them in a "stream of consciousness" way without reflection, which I find to be more truthful.

When I'm finished writing and reread what I have, I often find myself asking, "Do I believe that?" I then feel rejection because I don't want that to be true. With it staring me in the face and knowing that I was as honest as I could be, I create a great starting point for new beliefs and the motivation to adopt them.

If you carry the exercise all the way through and find that it takes a little too long to do ten times in a single day, then reduce the number of times rather than do the exercise incompletely.

The value of this practice comes from two places:

1. You get in the habit of regularly stepping outside yourself and honestly identifying the beliefs that form the current context of stuck-ness, limitation, or fear.

2. You get in the habit of being able to be honest quickly, without a bunch of guilt and noise about what you are thinking and feeling, which allows you to approach change more effectively.

Committing to start, picking small things that are less daunting, and going through the whole exercise is a great training activity. Your skill will build quickly.

You will then be able to move rapidly to changing more critical limiting beliefs that create a more significant shift in your life.

As long as you work in situations where you have feelings that indicate you are stuck with limiting beliefs, then every success matters. You are creating a lifelong habit that will give you power that you cannot yet imagine.

Another lesson from the piano years was that students who practiced every day for 30 to 45 minutes made far more progress than those who practiced hours and hours but only on the weekend.

This is true across every discipline. Small periods of consistent practice each day create better retention and more effective skill mastery than long periods of practice spaced further apart.

For this reason, the assignment to identify your triggers and practice identifying limiting beliefs, picking new ones, and changing your context must be done every day for maximum effectiveness.

Remember the principle of fun. Could you make it a game? Avoid getting trapped in the spiral of self-criticism when you make lists of beliefs you find unattractive.

As you do this more frequently and more effectively, the small changes you begin with will soon get larger, and the growing realization that you have the power to shape your life will create motivation.

Chapter 21

USING CONTEXT TO MASTER A SITUATION

A ll of us have situations where we know we haven't demonstrated our best behavior. We didn't put our best foot forward. We reflect ruefully in retrospect that we screwed something up. Then we stew in uncertainty about what to do next.

This often happens because we have come to a situation with a pile of limiting beliefs and a context that looks more like a small prison cell.

Some examples are below. Please read carefully and reflect on where you have opportunities.

- A work situation where you feel intimidated by a colleague or by your boss.

- A situation with your life partner where something got out of hand.

- A family member or friend where a simmering dispute has created a level of ongoing tension that makes every interaction uncomfortable.

- A child where the communication is strained, and you feel like you have no idea what to do to get back on track.

- A presentation to deliver at work.

- A speaking engagement where you will be in front of an audience of 100 people.

- A commitment you made to a friend to go somewhere or do something.

- A choice you made to start a new sport or learn a new skill, and you're terrified, you will look stupid.

Please take a moment now to think of a situation that is coming up for you in the next few days, where you have that awful feeling in your stomach because you don't know how to handle it. Every time you think about it, you put it out of your mind because you don't know where to start.

The previous exercise was to stop during the day when you feel awkward about something "in the moment," and then write down those beliefs, make changes and decide what to do differently. For a situation that exists in the future, you need some small variations.

Don't rush this. Your habits will tell you to brush it off or hide it "for later." If this situation is important to you, then it is worth investing time to create an entirely different context based on different beliefs. Then you will have the power to create success.

As we do this, there are several things to remember.

- You cannot control the behavior of another person.

- You have no idea what another person is thinking.

- If you think that all someone else has to do is think about you, that is arrogant and wildly mistaken. People are far more consumed in worrying about their own stuff.

- You have enough work to do by focusing only on your own beliefs and context.

- If you focus only on what you control, you will have far more success than if you worry about others' comments, attitudes, imagined thoughts, or potential outcomes.

- Each situation is an experiment. Especially in the beginning, focus on being truthful with yourself, patient with the process, and what you are learning.

- Even if you go through the following exercise and the situation doesn't work out exactly as you want, the experience will give you the tools to behave more calmly and powerfully in subsequent situations.

With these facts firmly in mind, let's get started.

- List the people and parameters you believe are difficult about the upcoming situation.

- Carefully consider and list why you believe each thing represents a difficulty.

- List what has occurred in the past to create your perception of difficulty.

- Honestly assess each difficulty as a fact or belief.

- As a tool to help with the previous step, consider whether an independent observer of the situation would agree with your assessment, or if a belief colors you.

- Write down all the beliefs that you have about the situation or person.

- Ask yourself, "What else *could* I believe?"

- Describe what you would do if the new belief were true.

- Describe what you think would happen if you took that new course of action.

- Continue this process until you have eliminated anything that flows from negative assumptions about the other person or situation, negative assumptions about yourself, or beliefs that are unfounded in objective fact.

- Make firm choices about what you will say or do differently with the new context in place and explore how you feel.

- Check and see whether the fear or concern you have about the situation has changed. If it has, you have created a new context. If it hasn't, go back through the exercise and find out where you have missed important points.

Without exception, if you do this carefully and thoroughly, with complete honesty, you will uncover beliefs in your context that have no basis in fact. They may come from assumptions about others' opinions, gossip at the water cooler, your background, or 100 other places.

These false beliefs contribute to misunderstanding, blindness, and deafness as we think about things facing us in the future. Ultimately this creates a continuation of fear and failure.

As you get good at this, it will become fun, and you will begin to laugh at yourself when you consider all the beliefs you carry that create the tiny prison of context where you used to live.

If you come from a place of love, forgiveness, and possibility instead of believing old stories of limitation, negativity, and lack, you will find situations far easier to negotiate and navigate, and an entire world will begin to open itself before your eyes.

A sense of gratitude and power will replace fear, and you'll realize more and more each day, the power you control to create your life.

After the situation unfolds, go through the exercise again and see what went well and what went awry. Make new choices about needed follow-up.

Chapter 22

USING CONTEXT TO MASTER YOUR DAY

L earning to use the power to create your context starts by recognizing situations where you have lived in a limiting context and then applying the steps from Chapter 21.

As you get more familiar and more comfortable with your context skill, you will want to live every day from the place of a powerful creator.

Mastering the skill of context creation will enable you to meet unexpected challenges without drama and give you the tools to quickly identify your barriers, change them, and move quickly through situations that previously caused problems.

In Chapter 17, I described seven essential keys to creating new beliefs. One addressed ritual. I also gave you a simple example of a morning ritual to begin the day more powerfully.

Most of the limiting beliefs that form a "context prison," which keeps us from creating a life that we want are centered around:

- What we believe we can do.
- What we believe we are worth.
- What we believe is possible for us to achieve.

As you practice creating context by addressing specific

situations, you will notice recurring themes in the beliefs that keep you stuck.

In creating a ritual to keep your whole day in a context of freedom, prosperity, and joy, you will need to address those recurring themes specifically.

For example, if you are aware of situations or conversations today that gave you trouble in the past, focus your morning meditation on creating a change in your beliefs.

You do this by declaring a new belief that expands your context and gives you power in a fearful situation. You declare it, repeatedly and clearly, to crowd out the voices of the past, which bring the all-too-familiar feeling of self-doubt.

Combining this with determining the assumptions and actions that flow from a context built from the new belief, you'll empower yourself in the morning for situations throughout the day.

One such ritual involves self-love. This is a delicate topic for many. I often hear people say that they can express great love for others, but they stumble and choke when they turn the spotlight inward.

This is a profoundly troubling illusion. A lack of self-love often shows up as an outpouring of attention on others. We do this to crowd out the self-doubt and to quiet voices of self-loathing. You then spend time and energy on others and often end up feeling empty, exhausted, and even resentful.

The truth is that you can't truly love others more than you love yourself. If you love and honor yourself, you will have more love for others, and you will find it invigorating, not exhausting.

This shows up starkly when we fall all over ourselves to keep our promises to others and rarely keep our commitments. The reason we don't keep commitments to ourselves is that we don't love ourselves. That may sound harsh, but it's true.

The obvious solution is to learn to love yourself. A simple test is to stand in front of a mirror and look deeply into your own eyes. Then say, gazing deeply into your soul, "I love you."

Many clients report this to be a tough exercise. They look away, feel anger or embarrassment or shame. They want to substitute any other word for "love." One told me that he would rather put his hand in a meat grinder than do this exercise.

The sad truth is this: because we intimately know about all our failings and all the times we did less than we committed, or even things we are ashamed of, our true emotion is a lot closer to loathing than loving.

If you want to create a context of power where you build the future of your dreams, this is the first thing that must change. Standing in front of the mirror and repeating "I love you" will real intent for 60 seconds might prove to be a daunting challenge at first. Do it anyway.

After the initial difficulty wears off, and you can say this repeatedly without looking away, check your heart. Check to see if you are genuinely focused and present or merely repeating words.

The next expansion of this vital practice is to say out loud the things that you do, which prove that you love yourself. This is not about self-indulgence. This is not the time to list all the stuff you bought for yourself or all the pleasures you gave yourself.

Often, we engage in such extravagance to try to prove something. We are trying to mask the fact that we do not like ourselves much, and we use external trinkets to hide the truth.

This is like a person in a relationship who does something mean or stupid and then thinks that buying flowers, chocolates, or clothing somehow erases the misdeed without fundamentally getting to the root of the problem.

Learning to wholeheartedly, truthfully, and sincerely love

yourself is the foundation of a powerful context for your life. When you begin thinking about what you do to demonstrate real love for yourself, it must consist of things that nourish your spirit and soul.

The fact that you meditate regularly or nourish yourself spiritually in a compelling way, in whatever fashion is appropriate, is one evidence of self-love.

The fact that you exercise regularly and take care of your body with proper nourishment and sleep and other self-care rituals is a demonstration of self-love.

Saying no to others' requests when they are not appropriate and in your best interest, is evidence of self-love. Letting people take advantage of you and stomp on your boundaries is not kind to them, and it is cruelty to you.

Creating a morning ritual that includes self-love is the essential first step in setting up a powerful day and then a succession of powerful days. Self-love is only the beginning. Even though this love is a crucial first step, there are many parts of a limiting context. Each must address each piece in turn.

- Perhaps you have lived in a world of pretense.
- Perhaps you lie regularly by telling people things are great when that is not true.
- Perhaps you exaggerate about the weekend because you want to sound impressive.
- Perhaps you pretend that you are hiding who you are.
- Perhaps you live regularly in the victim corner blaming everything around you.
- Perhaps you tell yourself that you don't matter.
- Perhaps you feel resentful of others' success.
- Perhaps... fill in the blank.

"How are you? I'm fine, how about you? Great, thanks." We've all had meaningless ritual conversations such as this. What else is possible as you create your new daily context of power?

There are indeed times where you should not share things about your life. It is also true that keeping things stuffed inside, thinking that nobody notices, no one cares or that no one can or would do anything, is harmful and contributes to the bricks in the walls of your "context prison."

If honesty is not something you struggle with, perhaps integrity is an issue. You can spot this problem if you regularly commit to things and then don't live up to your commitment.

The disconnect created by talking one way and living another creates an energetic dissonance that destroys your confidence, makes you feel like you have things to hide, and adds more layers to the beliefs that build your limiting context.

Don't be discouraged if things do not happen all at once. Building a meaningful daily ritual that gives you the power to identify and change limiting beliefs as they show up during your day is done gradually.

Start with self-love. Move on to other characteristics that you want to change. Include those choices and obligations in your meditation. Visualize real situations in your life where you behave differently based on new commitments that you make that morning.

Days pass quickly, and soon you will have evidence of significant changes in your life. You will begin to discard limiting beliefs about yourself. Even those limiting beliefs so deeply woven into your body that you don't even know they hold you captive.

Rejoice in every victory. Be patient and don't give up.

Chapter 23

USING CONTEXT TO MASTER YOUR LIFE

Getting good with your daily ritual will naturally lead you to think about how to show up powerfully in the world all the time.

When the real power of a new context begins to manifest itself in your life, you will be drawn to more significant questions that naturally flow from an expanded view of yourself and your possibilities.

- Who are you? Really?

- What are you about in the world? Really?

- What are your true possibilities? Really?

- How can you get where you want to be?

Regardless of your religious participation, most people have spiritual awareness. You came from somewhere else. You are fashioned from divine substance and wisdom. Underneath all the negative noise, you have infinite potential. You are a child of God.

Most people have not taken significant time out of the meaningless busyness that captivates most of our attention to sit and contemplate real answers to these questions. We don't *slow down* enough to genuinely connect with the spiritual plane we all know is there.

If you *knew* you had a divine origin and infinite potential, and that were your context, what assumptions would you make? What actions would flow from that context? Where are you today by comparison? Are there things you want to do differently?

We talked earlier about the value of making declarations. Even knowing that it's difficult to do. Why? Often when we make a resolution resolve, we don't believe it. We get assaulted with the history of past failures and our mountain of disbelief.

Even with the discouraging voices of the past, a firm and bold declaration carries power. Even if you no more than *desire* to believe what you have declared, that desire can drive you to create actions in support of your declaration.

Moving through those actions in support of your fledgling belief and powerful declaration will yield unexpected discoveries. Things will happen that you do not expect and could not have predicted.

Those occurrences will create evidence and proof that support your newly declared context. When this happens, belief grows, only because you now have mounting evidence.

This becomes a self-reinforcing cycle. More actions create more discoveries, which in turn generate support for larger beliefs and a more empowering context.

There are two benefits to this cycle. First, you strengthen the belief that you declared by seeing that these unexpected discoveries support the belief and the new context.

Second, the fact that it happened with *one* declaration is also evidence that it can happen *again* with another declaration and another. Suddenly, the power of the process becomes more evident.

You develop greater willingness and capability to engage in the process of re-weaving your context out of larger and more powerful beliefs. You are breaking down the walls of your self-imposed prison.

Declarations lead to actions. Actions lead to discoveries. Discoveries support what you are doing and give you the power and courage to repeat the process.

Over time, this constitutes the process of tearing out the underbrush, ripping up the weeds, and beating a new path through the forest.

By refusing to take the old path and requiring yourself to forge ahead in the new direction, again and again, even the most deeply held beliefs, those woven into the very cells of your body, can be changed.

This is the true meaning of "neuroplasticity." The actual capacity of the brain to rewire itself and create a new default response to replace the old one.

Rewiring your brain takes time and practice, and above all, persistence. Before the new pathway is completely worn, your natural tendency and habit will be to default to the old belief and behavior.

The very fact that you know this gives you a powerful advantage. Now you know to expect the immense pull of the old habit. The old way is just the natural way you learned to respond over the years or decades.

The new way will be a matter of consistent choice and insistent perseverance until it becomes established as the default mechanism for behavior in any given situation.

Most of us blindly move through life, giving free rein to those habits and beliefs that are ingrained so deeply in us we are unaware of them. This lack of awareness creates a context of impenetrable concrete and steel.

Making decisive choices, powerful declarations, and then taking the necessary action is the path to changing these things and blowing out the walls, one belief at a time.

In my quest to fulfill my highest purpose, three questions have helped me create a context of unlimited vision and power. I also take clients through creating answers to these questions for their own context work.

The first question is, "Who Am I?" In considering this in the most significant way possible, I created a document and program I call the PTAC (Personal Truth and Commitment).

The Personal Truth and Commitment is a deeply personal and powerful journey connecting you to your divine origin and destiny and giving you language and power that inspires your heart every day, gives you patience and strength to deal with any adversity and keeps you fired up and vibrant as you find and fill your highest purpose.

The second question is, "What Am I Doing?" In considering this while setting up my context of freedom, I created the PDAC (Personal Declaration and Commitment)

The Personal Declaration and Commitment is a deeply personal and powerful discovery and choice allowing you to freely, openly, and fearlessly declared to yourself and the world what you value and your absolute commitment to creating something that lifts your light and serves those around you.

The third question is, "How Will I Do This?" In considering this in a broad enough scope to accomplish the declaration, I created the PPAC (Personal Plan and Commitment).

The Personal Plan and Commitment is a deeply personal and powerful evaluation and adjustment of how you use your time, attention and love, to eliminate distractions and stories and cultivate attitudes, habits, and practices that help you be your best self, fully serve those around you and fulfill your highest purpose.

These three documents form the basis of my infinite context and allow me to move through the world the way that I want to. I created them using precisely the processes I describe in this book.

When you dream big, declare audaciously and act purposefully, sometimes you succeed, and sometimes you fall flat on your face. Both in creating these guides and in trying to live them, failure and recommitment was a regular part of my process.

When that happens, you can get down on yourself very quickly. The pull of the old limited context becomes a siren song of great attraction. "Why don't I just go back like I was?" Quitting is always an option, but if you do, you lose momentum and reinforce the "truth" of the old context.

The answer is forgiveness – forgiveness of your own mistakes and those of others. Because I struggled most of my life mightily with "I am fundamentally flawed," the principle of forgiveness, discussed in Chapter 17, has become an essential ingredient of my daily life.

I dare greatly and declare greatly, and I invite you to do the same. Knowing that we fail regularly and cannot with even moderate perfection live up to these declarations, the principle of forgiveness and recommitting is essential to creating a true infinite context. The alternative is to shrivel up and settle for the small version of yourself.

One final tool has to do with our perceptions of time. One of the most frequent complaints and constraints I hear about is, "I don't have enough time." That is absolute nonsense. You have an infinite amount of time.

What you lack is the discipline to use your time the way you want to. You have not trained yourself to say "no" to distractions. Instead, you spend the time you have focused on things that are not truly important to you.

If you live in the prison of a context created by old habits and beliefs, then "lack of time" becomes just one more way that you let Fear, Procrastination, and Self-Sabotage thwart the realization of your true possibilities.

To solve this problem, I created the picture you see on the next page (figure 1). It's called "The Alchemists Formula to Create Time." This diagram shows exactly how to create all the time you want. You find Time at the nexus of Purpose, Power, and Skill.

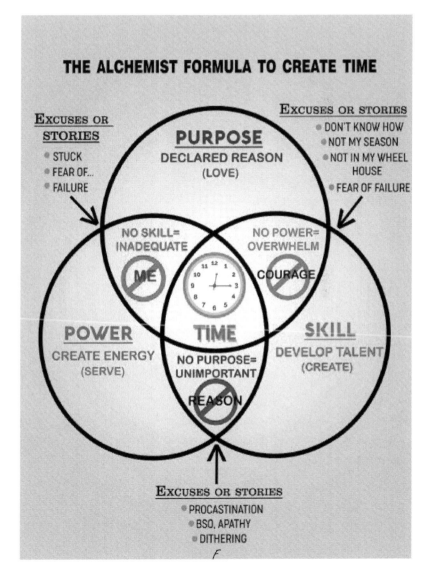

Figure 1. The Alchemists Formula to Create Time

If you have a mission that fulfills your declared and deeply held purpose, and you have the energy you are willing to devote to that thing, and you have a skill that comes from developing talent, then you find the time and complete that mission.

You learn to say no. You no longer allow the urgent needs of others to determine your priorities. You eliminate other activities that used to be attractive — your sense of what is important changes until you have a singular focus on your mission.

You then examine all the other things in your life and make a choice to sacrifice whatever else you might be doing so you can create the energy to make your commitment happen.

You already know what I mean. You have already had experiences in your life where you had something you were going to complete no matter what. You did whatever was required to find the power. The fact that you said you were going to complete it *no matter what* indicated the depth of your resolve and purpose.

If you were clumsy at doing whatever was required, you researched and practiced it until you developed the skill to the degree necessary to make it happen.

This may have been something you did to fill your highest purpose, or it may have been something you decided to learn for fun. Here are a couple of examples — one for fun and one tied to the core purpose of my life.

When I decided to learn snowboarding at age 45, I just decided it was going to happen. It had nothing to do with my life purpose, but it is an interesting example of this principle.

I took multiple weekends in a row, hired a personal instructor, instructed him to coach me hard until I learned the fundamentals. Then I practiced relentlessly, ignoring fatigue and some degree of injury until I acquired some level of excellence.

I did not "have time" to do this. However, my purpose, power, and skill combined in such a way that the time created itself.

Things were sacrificed to create a budget to accommodate the lessons. I developed the skill – learned how to snowboard, thereby accomplishing the goal.

Something as inconsequential in the grand scheme as learning to snowboard turned into a perfect example of creating time.

On a serious note, writing this book is another example. I had a miraculous visit with God at the doorway between life and eternity while I was unconscious and on life support for two weeks in a hospital ICU in June 2018.

I was given this book in one of these "conversations at the door," and I was instructed to write it. I did not have time to do that. My calendar was already packed from morning to night for the foreseeable future. There was just no way this was going to happen.

The conversation with God changed everything. The purpose was then apparent. My declared reason was the love that I feel for every person who is striving to overcome insurmountable barriers.

The power was the drive to complete the commitment I made in those conversations with God. The drive to honor that commitment created overflowing energy to work nonstop until both this book and the book *Meeting God at the Door* was done.

I already had skills in writing. I have written and edited many books and have been a good writer for most of my life. Gratefully, that was one thing I did not have to learn to do.

Above, I outlined two completely different examples where "lack of time" could have prevented these results or goals. I intentionally used examples at the opposite end of the spectrum from inconsequential, like snowboarding, to near-death experiences and conversations with God.

Most of what we do in life falls in between these extremes, and precisely the same principles play out exactly as diagrammed and can empower you to create the time you think you do not have.

The diagram also shows the way we get stuck. In the area where you have purpose and power but no skill, we create excuses and stories. Fear of failure due to lack of ability keeps us stuck. Ultimately you feel inadequate; there is something "wrong" with you.

In the area where you have purpose and skill but no power, the excuses change. "I do not know how." "It is not my season." A sense of overwhelm keeps you in a state of inaction, and again nothing happens.

In the area where you have power and skill but no purpose, then the stories change again, but the outcome is the same. Nothing happens. The stories are about procrastination, dithering, apathy and what some call the "Bright Shiny Object" (BSO) disease.

When all three are present, you create time. You create enough time to do anything you want to do and create anything you want to create.

My three keywords for the three areas of the diagram are Love. Create. Serve. Those three words guided my life and were my guides as I created my PTAC, PDAC, and PPAC.

I share these personal details, so you know that I came from a place of not having any of this to start with and having to create it all. There is nothing particularly special about me. You have the same divine origin and capability as I do. The choice to do the work to blow out the walls of your "context prison," rests with you.

As you do this, the journey itself creates a more extensive and broader field of vision and makes you more committed and powerful.

Like every form of growth, this journey takes place in stages. There is no need to fear or to imagine that you cannot make this happen. Even the very story, "I can't do this," is a function of the limiting beliefs of your present context.

You have the same choice right now you have always had, and that each of us has. Stay trapped in your present context or start on the road to blowing out the walls of your prison and creating the infinite context of your most cherished dream.

Chapter 24
FINDING THE GIFT

Regardless of the diligence and effort you put into the work of changing beliefs and reweaving your context, discouragement and setbacks are part of the journey.

I am sure you have noticed that every time you make a firm declaration and commitment to accomplish a new goal, things break, you get sick, people get ornery, or any number of things happen that get in the way.

I am sure you have asked yourself more than once if the universe is somehow conspiring against your good intentions and trying to stop you.

Know that you are not alone. It happens to everyone all the time. Every time you want to make a change for the better, the habits of the past and the inertia of change stand in the way.

This illustrates a principle called "Spiritual Gravity." It is the energetic analog of the physical gravity that keeps us all standing up. We all understand physical gravity. Gravity is that property that makes a 100-pound barbell heavy. We depend upon it to maintain order in our lives and to keep things sitting where they belong.

If gravity was not constant, then taking one step would be so complicated you couldn't move your foot, and the next step might bounce your head off the ceiling. We couldn't live in a world where gravity was not dependable and constant.

Every building we build, our cars, airplanes and every other form of transportation along with everything about our modern lives would instantly fall apart without predictable and dependable gravity.

If you are a person who's ever needed to lose weight, you also depend on gravity. Even if we wish gravity didn't tell us we were 50 pounds overweight, we depend on its certainty and regularity to allow us to lose weight and measure our progress while we do it.

The pull of gravity is the very thing that makes us sweat when we lift weights, ride our bike or do whatever we do to get back in shape.

Spiritual Gravity is the same thing. It is the natural resistance that exists when we try to push our character or our lives to a new place in contravention of existing habits.

Just like lifting weights develops our muscles, pushing against the spiritual resistance to change creates energetic muscles that are more developed and then available for our use.

The bigger the change you try to accomplish, the harder the gravity pushes back. This is true in weightlifting and personal development. The key for me has been learning to accept the challenge of making a change, especially changes involving a deeply held belief.

The resistance to your context changes is normal and important. It develops your character, persistence and "spiritual muscles." Spiritual gravity or resistance is a gift.

The most powerful tool I have discovered to overcome the discouragement of setbacks, disappointments, and failures is to "Look for the Gift." Every time something difficult happens, I have trained myself to ask, "What Is the Gift?"

I even looked for the gift in my recent life-threatening illness. That event cost me a month in the hospital and months of slow physical recovery. Shortly after regaining consciousness and realizing how long I had been out, the prognosis for recovery and how long it was going to affect my life, I asked myself this question, "What is the gift in this unexpected and life-changing event"?

In such a time, the gifts are not immediately apparent. I sat with the question for a while and as the days passed I began to have a long list of gifts that had come from that ordeal.

The answers that came were personal and powerful. As you ask yourself to search for and identify gifts in your setbacks and struggles, your answers will also add to your reservoir of determination and strength.

As you give yourself entirely to the process of creating new beliefs and an infinite context where anything is possible, you will feel an intense appreciation for the gifts that come from setbacks.

Things that others find negative, upsetting, and frustrating will be a joy to you. You will realize that they contribute to your ability to change your beliefs and context faster and faster.

Remember that every event is merely an event. The power of an event comes from the meaning we assign to it. If we decide something is negative or troublesome, then the consequences feel frustrating and unpleasant.

If you choose, and it is your right to choose, that everything is a gift, then the consequences are positive and uplifting. Especially with events that you cannot influence or change, it is better to find the gift and live in an uplifting and empowering context than in a context of frustration and negativity.

As with every piece of the puzzle, your personal choice is the fundamental key that belongs to you and cannot be taken away.

Choose wisely. Find the gift.

Chapter 25
PERSONAL DEVELOPMENT PUSH-UPS

In the world of sports or other accomplishments that depend on strength, agility, and the physique of the person involved, no one imagines that watching videos or reading books creates the necessary strength, agility or skill.

However, in the world of personal development, we think that watching YouTube videos, reading books, and going to conferences, if we do it enough, will create the needed growth. Somehow all this input will fix everything.

In my snowboarding example, the idea that I could watch a bunch of cool snowboarders do amazing things and suddenly, somehow, have the skill to even get down the mountain without falling on my face is laughable.

Reading personal development books is excellent. Watching YouTube videos of those who work in the field and are making powerful discoveries, can be motivating and exciting. Going to conferences and listening to well-known speakers can provide us with breakthroughs and insight.

Breakthroughs, insights and "aha" moments happen when we *learn* a new piece of truth. Accomplishment and skill happen when we *stay true* to what we have learned.

This is worth repeating. Write it on the wall and in your heart. Accomplishment and skill happen when we *stay true* to what we have learned.

Being true to what we learn means that we have to do our "Personal Development Push-ups."

I have a client who owns a gym. This particular gym is not one of the 24-hour fitness types where they oversell memberships and fill the room with lots of equipment that is rarely used.

Instead, this gym is for serious weightlifters who dedicate countless hours to their craft and then participate in bodybuilding competitions.

Someone who buys a membership to the gym does it because they have a particular goal. Often, they have a competition some months away they are training for.

They already have a training program, or they hire a trainer. In that process, they commit themselves to do what is required to meet the objective. If they do the work, they get closer to the goal and have a chance of winning the competition they plan to enter.

If they start and then quit, slack off in the middle, or pretend they don't have to do all the work, then the likelihood of success evaporates quickly.

All aspects of personal development work are the same. Just like with bodybuilding, there is internal and external work required.

The internal work requires discipline and courage. The external work requires hours and uncompromising dedication. Both are needed to create the result you want.

Changing the beliefs that are in your context, particularly those that are so deeply woven into your body that you respond without thinking, takes a significant amount of work. I have said that repeatedly in this book. Even though it's obvious, it still gets get ignored or minimized.

There is no shortcut to the work required to chop a new path through the forest. There is no automatic or easy way to overturn beliefs that have created habits in you that are years and even decades in the making.

However, with dedication and commitment, it can be done. You can eliminate every single habit and belief that does not serve you and does not align with the true nature of your divine capability.

You can create new habits and beliefs to replace the old ones and weave a new context that is empowering, ennobling, and ultimately wholly satisfying.

I have given several examples of exactly how to do this. I have described how I have done it and how I teach clients to make these critical and life-changing adjustments.

My deepest desire for you is that you understand that you have the capability, starting right now, to make these changes in your life.

No matter where you have been, no matter what has happened to you, no matter what your situation is right now, you can start the process today.

It is one of the defining characteristics of human beings that we have this divinely given ability to choose, return to the simplicity, curiosity, excitement, and belief of childhood, and create an amazing future.

Your only limits are your imagination and those beliefs you choose to keep.

Remember that you are in the process of re-training your brain. As you do all the personal development work required, remember that the habits stored in your mind and your body will push back.

Ultimately, you have control of your brain and can overcome all this resistance. It takes discipline. Some people hate that word. Remember that discipline is just reminding yourself of what is important.

Stay focused on the opportunity. All around you are books like this, as well as videos, and stories of people who made the very decisions I refer to, and have undertaken the rocky road to get where they want to go and have succeeded. Many then tell the story of the journey.

It's easy to ignore these stories as either exaggerated, "good for them, but I could never do this," or as outright lies. Then you can utter some dismissive comment and return to your rut.

You can always stay in your rut. No one can deny you that. No one can deny your great victory if you make a choice and then make it happen.

Even though I have given many examples and suggestions in this book, it will be your creativity and perseverance that takes these principles and creates the best way for you.

Your path is your path, and you must decide what it looks like and how fast you choose to walk it. There isn't any "wrong" way to do this except not to start. Start today.

The last thing to remember is this. This saying was written in my heart most forcefully from a scene in *Star Trek VI The Undiscovered Country*. If you are not a "Trekkie," you won't remember this, but you will get the picture.

If you are, you remember the scene where the Klingons had captured Captain Kirk, had a mock trial and sentenced Kirk to life in an alien labor camp. He was trying to figure out how to escape, as usual.

An alien creature approached him and asked, "do you want to get out of here?" Kirk responded typically, "there's gotta be a way."

I assure you, that no matter where you are, "there's gotta be a way."

Chapter 26

GETTING HELP

Next to a firm commitment to change your context, the most critical part of this total journey is getting the right help.

You didn't create the context you have today by yourself. The input of parents, friends, religion, society, culture, school and a myriad of experiences shaped how you view the world and, more importantly, what you believe is now possible.

Trying to change your context, especially if you want significant change, will be much, much faster with a support system on which you can depend. Creating this support is critical to your success.

I am blessed with a life partner that is interested, committed and supportive. You may or may not have that blessing in your relationships, family or friends. I have hired many coaches who have helped and mentored me. I have turned to God for unfailing strength.

Whatever you must do to create a support system, do it. Once again, it is critical. The work can be difficult. Habits can be overpowering; Old stories may seem like absolute truth.

Sometimes we feel like we must do everything on our own. Sometimes we feel like we don't want to discuss beliefs and their consequences because we might be embarrassed or look stupid.

Sometimes we may doubt that we are worth the effort or that

we really will succeed. Be assured; you are worth every investment of time, energy and cash required to create the life you want.

You are not alone, and you are not that different from others, making the same choices. As a coach, I deal every day with beliefs that keep people locked behind prison doors of their own making.

Without difficulty, I can see the great opportunity that lies currently just beyond their reach. It would be within reach if they would discard the weight created by a context woven from old stories and beliefs.

One of the most rewarding parts of my work is to see the joy and success that come when people shed old stories and embrace the new truth that is empowering and creates amazing growth right before their eyes.

As you start on this journey, get the help you need.

- It keeps you from being discouraged.
- It keeps you from suffering too much from your blind spots.
- It keeps you focused on your dreams.
- It helps you stay clear on your most significant changes.
- Above all, it keeps you strong and reminds you that the truth you are aiming for is possible.

If the things I have talked about in this book seem like they would help *you*, there is information in the appendix about how to reach me and have a further conversation.

Whether you seek my help or that of another, if this book has kindled the desire in you to reach beyond your current limits, tear out the walls of your old context and create a new framework of freedom, prosperity, and joy because of your divine nature and true opportunity, then do it.

Do it now. Every day you delay increases the power of the old walls a little bit more. One more day goes by and then one more year.

Your opportunity and destiny await.

Go for it.

"What is love unless you share it?

What is tenderness unless you show it?

What is kindness unless you give it?

Share it, Show it, Give it."

Kellan Fluckiger

EPILOGUE

Looking out your window, you see a peaceful scene. Whether you live in a busy city or an idyllic setting in the country or on the seashore, you feel peace in your heart.

The circumstances of your life bring you joy and contentment. These circumstances are of your creation and are precisely what you want to have.

Every day you rejoice in your opportunity to love and serve those around you. You live without stress and in full control of your schedule, your creativity, your relationships, and every other aspect of your life.

You have abundance in every facet of your existence. You reflect in sincere gratitude about the opportunities that are before you right now.

You also remember the context that used to represent the limits of your freedom, prosperity, and joy. You now understand how transparent and temporary those seemingly concrete barriers were.

Rejoicing in what you have created, you can't help but wonder what the next phase of growth will bring. You don't know exactly, but the uncertainty is not unsettling.

You know that whatever the next level is, it will bring joy and contentment as you once again explore your context and pursue your opportunity for endless expansion.

APPENDIX AND CONTACT INFORMATION

For access to the resources I've talked about in this book, they are on my website at www.kellanfluckiger.com.

- *Tightrope of Depression* is available in paperback, hardcover and digital (Kindle). This #1 best-seller is the first in a trilogy. The second book, *Down from the Gallows* is due spring 2020.

- Meditation Books – Volume I in my 5-part series is *Meditation, The Amazing Journey Within* are on Amazon in both Kindle and paperback and is directly mentioned in this book. Four additional volumes on meditation are also available in both paperback and Kindle.

- Meditation music – there are many apps available for smartphones. I wrote a piece called *Inner Sanctum: Circles of Peace*. A sample of this music is available for free on my website.

Information on creating effective and powerful morning rituals, including Spiritual, Physical, Emotional, and Mental components, and especially the powerful self-love components is part of my *Results Equation Intensive* program. More information is available at www.resultsequationsintensive.com.

To speak with me about creating your Personal Truth and Commitment Statement (PTAC) and the other parts of that framework or to learn more about coaching and the work I do with individual and corporate clients, you will need to provide your name, email address, and phone number before booking an appointment.

I frequently use social media as a platform to discuss everything in this book and other coaching processes that I use. Follow me on Facebook at www.facebook.com/kellan.fluckiger3

I've created a free video series to help you get unstuck, stop procrastinating, end self-sabotage, and get you moving on your way to success, prosperity, and happiness. You'll find them on my YouTube channel – Ultimate Life Formula (or search by my name).

ABOUT THE AUTHOR

Kellan Fluckiger is the author of the #1 best-selling book *Tightrope of Depression*, an in-demand speaker, and highly successful coach. Working with CEOs of companies large and small, Kellan has touched and transformed many lives over the past 30 years.

A certified master coach and former C-suite Executive, Kellan has coached everyone from Super Bowl winners to music award winners and everyone in between.

Kellan is a master at high achievement. As a motivational speaker and business coach, his journey has benefited thousands. He has written five books on meditation and provides coaching and support for creative's, entrepreneurs, and leaders on their journey through struggles and victories as they discover, develop and deliver their talents to the world.

In addition to coaching, Kellan has written, recorded, and produced 11 albums of original music. He's been running a successful recording studio for over 35 years. Samples of Kellan's music are available on his website at www.kellanfluckiger.com.

Born in San Francisco, CA, Kellan now spends most of the year creating and writing in Canada with his wife, Joy, and their two cats and two dogs Popcorn and Cooper.